Blossoms on a Rooftop

Luba Czerhoniak Fedash

DORRANCE PUBLISHING CO., INC.
PITTSBURGH, PENNSYLVANIA 15222

Dedication

To my wonderful, patient husband of 44 years, John, who supported me throughout this very important project; to our pride and joy daughters, Kyra and Laura, and their loving families; to the "Lemko" People everywhere.

Acknowledgment

My sincere "thank you" to Professor Paul Robert Magocsi, Chair of Ukrainian Studies at the University of Toronto, for his genuine interest, overall help, encouragement and support in favor of publishing my story, "Blossoms on a Rooftop".

The events, people, places, and dates, herein are depicted to the best recollection of the author, who assumes complete and sole responsibility for the accuracy of this narrative.

ISBN-10: 0-8059-7099-1
ISBN-13: 978-0-8059-7099-9
Library of Congress Control Number: 2005934762

Printed in the United States of America

First Printing
For more information or to order additional books, please contact:
Dorrance Publishing Co., Inc.
701 Smithfield Street
Third Floor
Pittsburgh, Pennsylvania 15222
U.S.A.
1-800-788-7654
www.dorrancbookstore.com

Contents

*Luba at age 7 in
her homeland*

*Photo taken in 1955, before
the rest of our family came to
America. Left to right: Luba,
Mother Tekla and Father John*

*One and only photo my father
had of our (his) family during
the many years of separation.
Left to right: Brother Michael,
Mother, brother John and in the
center, Luba at age three or four*

Purpose

The anticipation of going back to the neighborhood of my beginnings on this side of the ocean filled me with excitement as well as suspense. Forty-some years have passed since I left 57 Greene Street in Jersey City, and I have not been back. Over the years I often thought about the tiny three-room, third-floor apartment where I spent the last years of my teens: its surroundings, especially the boxed-petunia garden on the neighbor's rooftop which kept my spirit alive during those difficult first years in America; getting to know the father I didn't remember; renewing my relationship with my immigrant mother when she joined us a couple of years later; learning the basics of the English language: being exposed to unfamiliar customs....

Upon my return to the neighborhood of my youth, I expected changes, but never a complete makeover! Sadly, my fervent wish to physically replicate the mental image of my first home in America through this visit, and recapture a moment from the life of the bewildered sixteen-year-old me, was not to be. After some consideration and yes, shock, I arrived at a solution as to the preservation of my memories, still clearly defined in my mind. Was this moment the catalyst that gave birth to a dream which would eventually result in a book called *Blossoms on a Rooftop*? Probably, but not entirely. There were other catalysts which helped pave the way to the realization of this dream, as well.

I hold fond memories of another place now alive only in my heart—the place of my birth whose soil claims my roots, childhood memories, and much of whom I am today! That place no longer exists on the physical level, either, but in the hearts of the Lemkos in exile and those fortunate enough—like myself—to have immigrated to America, our homeland, Lemkovyna, amidst the serene Carpathian Mountains, will remain loved and remembered for as long as life itself lasts. For me, this innocent loss of the Lemko homeland further solidified the need to write my story.

My memoirs would not be complete without a mention of the emotional impact the devastation of the City of Glogow (Glogau), following the Second World War, had on my young mind. I went to school in Glogow after the forced deportation from our Lemkovyna in 1947. How well I still remember the forlorn land blanketed by jagged cement boulders and, here and there, a lonely, badly damaged structure hanging in midair; skeletons of some victims still resting on the windowsills. I am sure those ruins are now a part of past history, and the city of rubble I lived in has returned to its pre-war splendor and glory. But is my mind ready to let go of the painful memories completely and make room for the present-day reality? Not willingly! The worst of them continue to harass me to this day, usually in the form of nightmares, though with less frequency and power with each passing year. Time does heal wounds, but only to a degree....

I hope the sharing of my memories and experiences with you, dear reader, will enrich your life, as it has mine, telling you my story.

A Brief History

The two-room humble log dwelling in the foothills of the Carpathian Mountains in the southeast corner of present-day Poland was home to several generations of my paternal side of the family. I was born in that home on May 10, 1933, and it served as my place of refuge up to the age of fourteen. It might have remained such for years to come, had it not been for the unthinkable that caused its untimely demise....

Seventy-some log homes similar to the one my family and I lived in made up our ancestral village called Liszczyny (Leezh-chy-ny). The village was named after a hazelnut bush (liszczyny) abundant in the area. Our village of Liszczyny (Leszczyny) was one of countless other similar villages scattered over the foothills of the Carpathian Mountains, which in totality became known as the Lemko region, or simply Lemkovyna. Each village boasted its own—pride and joy— onion domed—church enhanced by intrinsic interior designs and beautiful icons.

The name Lemko was derived from an expression, *lem*, which means "only," (ex. *lem toto, lem tamto*, meaning "only this and only that"). The word *lem*, used generously by the people in their unique language, unknowingly earned them the name "Lemko," or "Lemkovyna" when reference is made to the region itself.

Through the years the Lemkos were also known by various other names: Carpatho-Rusyns, Rusnaks, Uhro-Rusins, Carpatho-Russians, Ruthenians, Carpatho-Ukrainians or simply Slavic. The varied names were probably the result of the changing borders and the political situations in whichever neighboring country that occupied the

Lemko-Rusyn region at any given period in history. To that effect, I can relate one interesting fact from my own life. My paternal grandfather and I were both born in the same log home on the same bed and on the same piece of land, yet we were each born in different countries—he in Austria-Hungary and I in Poland. In spite of the Lemkos' diversified names and countries of origin over the centuries, the people themselves remained the same, perpetuating their own distinct language, their own religion, and their own down-to-earth culture, similar to their Slavic (or other) neighbors', yet distinctly their own, even though they never had a country to call their own.

And who were/are these people known throughout history by different names: the Lemkos, the Carpatho-Rusyns, the Lemko-Ukrainians…? Where did the original settlers (exact dates unknown) come from? Or what peril at the time drove them to seek refuge in the wilderness of the Carpathian Mountains? And what was so special about this desolate place that motivated them to settle there, in spite of the hardships and dangers they must have encountered in a land parts of which might never have been trod by a human foot? Was it the peace, the freedom, or the unique natural beauty that captured their spirits and impelled them to call these mountains their home?

There are no clear-cut answers to these important questions. History books past and present offer speculative answers at best, based mostly on verbal stories passed down from one generation to the next. In recent years, however, some beautifully illustrated and narrated books as well as articles have sprung up which offer valuable, sought-after information regarding the Carpatho-Rusyns or the Lemko-Rusyns or just Lemkos (all the same people). The two books I have read and highly recommend are entitled *"Our People"* and *"Carpatho-Rusyns,"* both written by the renowned historian of our people, Professor Paul Robert Magocsi. Today one can also obtain valuable information concerning the Lemkos, the Carpatho-Rusyns etc. on the Internet.

In my case, however, the knowledge regarding my ancestry—the Lemko-Rusyns—is first-hand experience. A memory sanctified by the passage of well over sixty years time, longing to be set free at long last so it can be passed on in hopes of further strengthening the legacy and perpetuity of this special group of people, a memory that encompasses not only the years from my birth to age fourteen spent on the homestead of my ancestors in the Carpathian Mountains, but also the years that followed. A sequence of events that led me far away from my homeland, first to a strange land in western Poland as a result of forced evacuation, and then to a father who in reality was a stranger to me in a strange land called America. A chronicle of challenges, hardships, and struggles, sprinkled with adventures and joys, many twists and turns as I traveled the highway of my life set before me by my destiny. A destiny which gave me the freedom and an opportunity to pursue and realize most of my goals and dreams, in my adopted country of America, which I came to love unconditionally and with all my heart, while still respectfully and affectionately remembering the land of my beginnings—the serene Carpathian Mountains of my youth.

The American Dream realized – Luba, John and their young daughters – Kyra, 9 and Laura, 6 years old.

The proud grandparents. From left to right: Grandma Luba, grandsons, Adam (16), Christopher (15), granddaughter, Kara (8), grandpa John and four-year-old Faith.

Chapter 1

Luba's Early Childhood

The premature birth of the visibly fatally ill baby girl shrouded the aged ancestral home with profound sadness and left the struggling infant's parents inconsolable in their grief. The self-taught village midwife who delivered the baby, small enough to fit in the palm of her father's hand, advised the family to accept the inevitable and forget about what might have been. She then took the baby away from her heart-broken mother and placed the ailing infant on the side to finish her brief life on earth in peace.

Several hours later, to the surprise of the devastated family, a squeak resembling a sightless kitten's cry in search of its mother's milk brought everyone in the house to their feet. The baby girl was not dying! She, like the newborn kitten, was hungry and wanted the feel of her mother's comforting arms and nourishment. This fortunate baby was me and my parents named me "Luba," which means "Love." My two brothers, Michael, nine, and John, six years old, jumped for joy because they now had a sister. My parents were jubilant that their second daughter (the first little girl, second in line, died at the age of two), was stubborn enough to cling to life in spite of all the odds against her. I refused to give up on the world even though the world gave up on me. My mother told me the story of my first few hours on earth many times during my growing-up years, usually to comfort me when nothing else seemed to work. My brothers also related what they remembered of my complicated birth, mainly when I angered them because I did something I was told not to do, or didn't do something I was told to do.

"To think we cried so hard when everyone said you were going to die when you were born," I heard them say, now and then.

"But I lived through it all and I am here to stay, like it or not!" I would answer.

On occasions, I would also receive spankings from one of them, and for no good reason I would always plead and demand an apology, which I seldom received. But in all fairness, I knew deep down my brothers loved me just as much as I loved them; we proved our love for each other many times over as children and later as adults.

My father left for America five weeks after I was born. At the time of my birth, he was already an American citizen and hoped to bring his entire family to his adopted country soon after my birth. Unfortunately, my mother's close ties to her own family interfered with his plans. To appease his wife (my mother), he made the journey back to America alone. He promised to return when he had earned enough money to make a better life for the family he left behind. And he kept his promise. He returned when I was about five years old. At home he found everything and everyone safe and sound, just as he had hoped he would.

Life was good! My father saved enough money from his hard work in America to build a bigger, more up-to-date home for his growing family. With the inherited farmland from his parents and the prolific forest, plus the additional acreage he purchased while living and working in America, his and his family's future would be secure. He felt certain his plans would meet all his expectations, and more. But would they? The merciless fate—like a thief in the night—put an end to all his dreams and aspirations before they even had a chance to be planted in the soil of his beloved Carpathian Mountains, on the homestead of his forefathers.

In September of 1939, Nazi Germany attacked Poland, followed by a Soviet invasion from the east three weeks later resulting in the disappearance of Poland as a country. When the two occupying powers divided Poland in October 1939, the Lemko Region in the Carpathian Mountains was left to the German sphere and became part of the Third Reich. My father's life as an American citizen living on Nazi-occupied land would, therefore, be placed in jeopardy—and possibly ours, too. When he was summoned to report to Nazi authorities for questioning, he knew he was left with only one option—leave his ancestral home and flee to his adopted country, where a part of his heart always stayed. The question was. Would he make it to America without being apprehended en route? He would have to take that chance for his own safety as well as his family's.

With tears in his eyes, an embrace for each of us, and a small knapsack on his back, he disappeared into the dark night, leaving behind his shattered dreams and broken promises to his loved ones. Not surprisingly, my mother had some explaining to do to the Nazi authorities about her husband's whereabouts.

"Why did your husband fail to report to the Authorities for questioning, and where is he now?" they wanted to know. She swore up and down she had no knowledge of her husband's whereabouts—and in a way she was telling the truth. To prove her point, she challenged the Nazi officials to search for him anywhere they wished—and they did. But, of course, they didn't find him. After several additional attempts, they gave up. Sadly, our home and family remained under surveillance for the duration of the Second World War.

I was too young to understand why our home suddenly changed from happy to sad. Why my kisses and hugs were not enough to make my mother smile and hug me back. Why my brothers no longer horsed around which always made me laugh. No one bothered to take time to explain to me, in simple terms, the reasons for all the changes. I wasn't even told why my father was no longer living with us. Or if he was ever coming back. This lack of understanding made me worry that I had something to do with the unhappiness which suddenly moved in on us, because on occasions I misbehaved. Of course, the picture became clear to me as I got a bit older.

I didn't spend enough time with my father during his short stay at home (only a few weeks) to really get to know him, miss him, or think about him, once he left for his former home in America. My memory of him was nothing more than a large puzzle with many missing pieces. To me he remained an enigma, someone who was in my life for a brief moment, not long enough to make a difference. As I matured, I thought about him more often, especially when I saw my peers enjoying great relationships with their fathers. I wondered what kind of man my own father was and how different my life might have been if he had been a part of it, or if he were to return.

There was one incident, however, during my father's brief stay at home that left a sketchy imprint in my mind. Our mixed-breed watch dog, Bingo, considered my father an intruder who was up to no good and needed to be removed from the property. Bingo had the run of our home and grounds. To show my father who was the master of the domain, he constantly barked, growled, and even showed off his sharp teeth when he spotted my father. Bingo was out to hurt him so he would go back to where he came from.

On one occasion, Bingo became adamant in showing off his dominance over this stranger once and for all. He raced towards my unsuspecting father, ready to attack. Seeing the danger my father was facing, I ran as fast as I could towards Bingo. I jumped on his back, knocked him to the ground and held his agitated face in my hands. I didn't fear him, because we were the best of friends. In the nick of time, I rescued my father from possible severe injury. And I had a few chosen words for my friend, Bingo. With his head still in my hands, I looked into his angry eyes and at the top of my voice, I reprimanded him, "Stop being so mean, you bad dog! Don't you know this man you were about to sink your teeth into is my father?" I do remember the incident, though somewhat fuzzily. Luckily, my family remembered the details of my bravery and concern for my father and kept it alive for me. According to them, Bingo listened and understood what I wanted him to know. He stopped treating my father as an intruder and accepted him as one of the family.

To fill the gap my father's absence left, I turned to my brothers for father figures, especially to my older brother, Michael, who was almost ten years older than I. Michael was my shining star, my role model, who in my eyes could do no wrong. He was the one I ran to when I needed comforting and my mother was not around; I went to John when I couldn't find Mother or Michael. I loved them both equally, though at different times for different reasons. I would have been devastated if one of them had suddenly disappeared into the dark night like my father did.

Over the years we wondered if my father made it to America or was apprehended on the way and put in prison, or worse yet, done away with. We wondered if we would ever see or hear from him again. My mother shed many tears and offered many prayers for his safety. We all prayed for some news from him, but there was none for as long as the war lasted, and beyond.

In spite of the raging war all around us, I still enjoyed a happy and carefree life for a time. Pauline, my best friend, and I continued to play for hours on end under the gnarled limbs of two ancient oak trees that had kept watch over our home for generations. We decorated our make-believe log cabin with wildflowers, abundant everywhere and different in every growing season. Barefoot, we chased each other over the rolling hills and valleys and challenged the bubbling brooks with our jumping skills. We were happy and too young to understand that nothing in life lasts forever. And that our carefree childhood days were about to end.

Sometime after my sixth birthday, the job of taking care of our three milking cows, previously shared by my two brothers, was handed over to me. My brothers were needed to farm additional land so our family could meet the steep assessments of farm products for war efforts. And this was the end of my carefree childhood days. My job began at sunrise and ended at sunset every day of the year except for Sunday mornings, the winter months, and a brief time I attended school. Restraining the cows by a rope made from our own home-grown and home-spun flax, I led them to the pastures far from home by the forest where I watched over them while they grazed all day. Overnight, I changed from a child enjoying childhood to a child with adult responsibilities, certainly beyond the scope of my six or seven years. But I was determined to live up to the trust my family placed in me. And I did!

Many an evening I barely made it home, too tired to walk to the house, let alone eat supper. My mother or one of my brothers would find me asleep on the hay in the stable next to the cows' stalls. I would be carried to the house and force-fed, not always successfully, because I was too exhausted to chew the food placed into my mouth and as a result would go into choking fits. In such cases, I was forced to drink some milk, not entirely by myself, either. The milk was poured into my mouth by one of my brothers—usually John—and all I had to do was swallow it. And it wasn't until I ate something or drank a glass of milk that I was allowed to sleep. Unfortunately, the morning usually always came much too soon, and I was awakened to start the routine over again. Was this child abuse? I believe in the twenty-first century it would be considered an abuse. But what did I know, or care, about such things? I did what I knew I had to do, and cared about things that brought joy into my otherwise mundane existence: the wonders of nature, minute and great, which never ceased to amaze me or lift my spirit then, and still do today!

Nature was my company as I watched over the grazing herd in my care, day in and day out, away from home and people. I made friends with trees and creatures on the ground and in the air. I gave names to the trees and talked to them. And I was convinced I heard them answer me back. I reprimanded the rabbits when I caught them munching on the neighbor's potato plants and cabbage heads, or birds when I caught them feeding on the golden waves of oats, wheat, or barley. And when the rabbits hopped away and the birds disappeared into the blue sky, I felt happy. I was sure they heard and understood me because my complaints were honored. I built log cabins of twigs— similar to the home I lived in—and imagined myself being a valued guest in different ones at different times. Wild berries in summertime represented fancy foods served by my make-believe hosts. And I learned to tell time by the sun shadows falling on the beaten paths in the villages of my creation. Some days I even talked to the sun, if I felt it wasn't moving fast enough toward the horizon, hence the reason for the long day.

On one occasion I came face to face with a big gray wolf. I didn't panic because I lived with nature and felt bonded with it. I talked calmly to the animal, like I did to every other wild creature. The wolf eventually walked away and left me and the grazing cattle unharmed. Wolves were known to do great harm to people and domestic animals, especially if they were hungry. Were the cattle and I spared because the wolf's belly was full, or because I spoke to him calmly and with utmost respect? The answers to these questions can only be speculative guesses, at best. The fact that I and the herd in my care came home that evening, unharmed, was nonetheless a miracle!

Since most of my waking hours were spent in the grazing fields, I looked upon my surroundings as my home away from home. Living in harmony with nature brought me satisfaction. And, for the most part, I was happy and glad to be alive, except on late autumn days when patches of frost covered the ground, or early spring days when rain fell from the sky non-stop all day, and I had to walk upon the cold earth barefoot, soaked to the bone. On those days I fed the soggy buttered bread in the pocket of my tattered jacket which was—my lunch—to my animal friends, because I didn't like the taste of watered-down buttered bread no matter how hungry I was. In such cases, I would tolerate the empty tummy and wait for our usual evening meal of potatoes and sauerkraut—that is, if I had enough strength left to chew and swallow a portion of it. I remember clearly to this day, how soothing my warm urine felt on my freezing feet and how welcomed it was each time nature called.

I also remember other autumn and spring days when everything was right with the world and I basked under the warm sun and ate my chunk of buttered oat bread with gusto, wishing I had more because it tasted so good. And all the discomforts of the past would quickly evaporate from my fledgling memory, like drops of dew from the blades of grass under the first rays of sun.

I was about eight or nine years old when the reality of war really touched my life where it hurt most—my heart. Out of nowhere Nazi soldiers appeared at our doorstep and ordered my mother to open the barn door for them. She knew better than to disobey their orders. My mother, brothers, and I watched in horror and disbelief as the soldiers unchained our one and only beautiful work-horse, Chestnut, and brazenly led him away. I tried running after them, yelling to give me back my Star, but was quickly pulled back by my mother and brothers.

"Get back here, Luba!" all three of them shouted.

"Do something, don't let them take my Star," I yelled back (Star was my pet name for Chestnut. I gave him that name because he had a perfectly formed star on his chestnut forehead).

"You have no right to take my Star!" I screamed at the soldiers. My mother quickly covered my mouth with both her hands to stop me from reprimanding the stern-looking armed soldiers.

"Don't you ever do that again!" Mother warned as tears streamed down from her frightened eyes. "You don't ever do or say anything that might anger the soldiers wearing the swastikas on their arms," she cautioned, and explained the meaning of that symbol to me—but not until the soldiers and my Star disappeared in the distance.

"Let them take anything they want, as long as they don't touch us," she stressed.

"Even my beautiful Star?" I cried.

"Even your beautiful Star, but not you, Luba, or your brothers."

"But how are we supposed to get along without Star?" I questioned tearfully.

"It won't be easy, and I don't have an answer to that question now. But I can tell you one thing for sure: As long as we are together and safe, we'll manage somehow. It's human life that's most important, so try everything to save yourselves until this ugly war is over," she said, as she looked at me and in the direction of my brothers.

I thought I understood what she was talking about. But did I really? I considered Star as one of us and no less human. He was my friend and I couldn't imagine life without him. When I wanted to ride him through the meadows on a Sunday morning in spring, summer, or autumn, a morning off from work for both of us, all I had to do was pull on his gorgeous mane and he would get down to his knees to make it easier for me to get on his back. And I thought I saw him lower himself to his knees as he was leaving us, but this time to say good-bye.

I promised my mother I would not act childishly next time the soldiers wearing the swastikas took something else from us, as long as they left us alone. But would they? I realized soon enough that losing my Star was only the beginning of what was yet to come.

Chapter 2

Luba's Recollections of the War

We heard about the destruction of the infrastructures in the distant and not so distant cities. We also watched in horror coal-black clouds streaked with red moving closer and closer to us, threatening at times to engulf our pristine Carpathian Mountains with their venomous fumes. "This is the end of the world," the village elders declared and urged the younger generation to repent "while there is still time." Fortunately for the world, the elders' predictions did not come to pass. It was Hitler and his evil regime that eventually ended, and our world became a better and safer place to live in because Hitler and his kind were no longer in it.

By the Grace of God, the Lemko Region remained relatively devoid of military action until 1944, when partisan activities increased and finally the arrival of Soviet troops and the massive campaign for control of the Dukla Pass (northeast portion of the Lemko Region) in the autumn of that year. But this is not to say the Lemko Region and its people sailed through this six-year-long war unscathed. Far from it!

The spring of 1943—the season of my tenth birthday—arrived with its usual glory and splendor, but for the hopelessly frustrated villagers who saw no end to this war the fury of winter raged on, in spite of the profusion of wildflowers, emerald-green grass, blooming fruit trees, and brushwood everywhere. These were trying times for me also, even though my love and devotion to nature, especially in spring, remained unchanged.

To keep the cattle from encroaching on the neighbors' property on the way to the pasture fields and back each day, they had to be restrained by a sturdy rope. Over time and from overuse, our one and only strong rope—a relic of the pre-war time—was becoming weak and prone to breakage. Fortunately, I knew how to tie a good knot and kept the rope in one piece for as long as it was possible. When the fibers that held the rope together, my day-to-day saving grace, became too fragile to hold additional knots and I saw it falling apart in front of my very eyes, I panicked! How would I be able to control the three unrestrained, rambunctious cows, harassed by super-size flies and mosquitoes, with appetites as huge as their stomachs and taste for the tender growing plants that people depended on for their own food? I worried. Asking Mother again for a new rope was useless. "Do the best with what you have, Luba. We can't afford to buy a new rope! And even if we could, such things can't be bought by civilians at this time." Her answer was always the same. In desperation, I turned to God for help. And He answered my prayers, but not in the way I expected.

On my way to the pasture fields one morning, I spotted two neighbor girls I knew (both around nineteen or twenty, like my brother Michael) in the underbrush in the ravine bordering our land. I was certain they saw me, but when I called them by their names, they not only ignored my call, they crawled further down into the bushes and purposely disappeared from my view. This strange phenomenon bothered me all day. What were those girls doing in that dangerous ravine at that early hour? Were they hiding from something or someone they feared more than the descent into an unfriendly ravine?

That evening on the way home, I witnessed an even stranger scene. This one frightened me half to death. Passing my aunt's house I saw several Nazi soldiers, armed with rifles, pushing and shoving my two first cousins, Mary and Anna (also Michael's age), out of their house. Their disheveled mother, my mother's sister Eugenia, was running after her daughters, and then in mid-stream changed her direction in pursuit of her two young sons in harm's way (John, about ten, and Peter, about eight years old) attempting a rescue operation on behalf of their sisters, while Anna and Mary pleaded to be released, to no avail. At one point, one of the girls managed to break loose and almost got away but was quickly apprehended, smacked across the face by the visibly irritated soldier, and forced to join her sister in the custody of the other soldiers. My distraught Aunt Eugenia was shouting blessings to her daughters while holding on to her two young sons for dear life. "God be with you, my children, and bring you back home safely," I heard her yell as her precious daughters were brazenly led away. But would she and the rest of the family be there for them, if and when they returned home? Time would tell!

Disregarding the delicate state of the knotted rope, I pulled on it as hard as I could and even cracked the whip in the air to urge the cattle to move faster, in an effort to beat the soldiers to our house. I hurriedly led the cows to their stalls, slammed the barn door behind me and ran to the house, hoping and praying I would find my family untouched by the Nazi predators. I barely stepped over the threshold and there was my frightened mother, ready to pull me in. She grabbed my hand and bolted the door behind us. Without a word from any of my family, I found myself sitting next to my brothers, huddled in the dark corner of the room. But, of course, there was no need for words. The actions of the Nazis in this case spoke louder than any words ever could.

Momentarily safe with my loved ones, my thoughts turned not only to my two first cousins who had been brutally taken away by the soldiers only minutes earlier, but also to the two neighbor girls I saw that morning hiding in the dangerous ravine. The answer to that dilemma was now clear. The girls were hiding to avoid being taken by the Nazis—God knows where and for what purpose. Mother hovered over the three of us like a mother bird over helpless fledglings in danger of being snatched away from under her by ravenous ravens if she as much as turned her head. She did not leave us until she was sure the Nazis were out of the village.

"They're gone for now! But I wouldn't be surprised if we see them here tomorrow again. And if not tomorrow, then a day or two after tomorrow," Mother sighed as she called the three of us to the table in the room lit by the light of the moon.

"We need to make some changes here and now, if we're going to survive this dreadful war," she said, nervously tapping her fingers on the table.

"What do you have in mind?" Michael asked, head bowed low.

"Drastic changes for all of us, but especially for you, Michael, because you're just the age they're after, it seems," replied Mother, brushing his hair away from his face. "John should be safe for now—they're not touching fifteen and sixteen-year-olds, yet," she said, her hand resting on his shoulder. "Anyway, I will need John to take over Luba's job."

I perked up! "And what will I be doing?" I wanted to know. The answer to my question was readily available. It seemed Mother had her plan all figured out.

"No child your age should have to be responsible for a job as enormous as I have in mind for you, Luba, but I have no choice in this, and I hope you can understand that." She squeezed my hand and went on. "Michael's life will depend—and in a way our lives, too—on how well you can keep the secret and do the job I am about to entrust to you."

What on earth is she talking about! I wondered. But I swore up and down, and I meant it, I would never reveal the secret, whatever it was, and would dedicate every minute of my life to save Michael's no matter what it involved. After all, Michael meant everything to me. Without Michael, life would be very, very sad. Over the years I had considered Michael my guardian angel on earth, and now that he needed me, whatever that need might be, I wanted to be his. Soon Michael's need for my help would be revealed.

For the next few hours that night we were busy preparing Michael's hideout. I held the kerosene lantern so Mother, Michael, and John could see into a dugout in the floor in the corner of the room. It had been used in the past for storing fruits and vegetables during winter months, since the root cellar was located away from the house, in back of the barn difficult to get to in waste-deep snow. How a tomblike hole that reeked with damp earth, rotten potatoes, turnips, carrots, and apples could serve as a hiding place for Michael was beyond me. But Mother knew best and we had to trust her judgment completely in this crises!

Once the accumulation of debris was removed from the intended hiding place, Mother found two old blankets and padded the damp floor in the hideout with them. Michael and John found a small bench Mother said our father had made years ago, and lowered it into the dugout for Michael to sit on. A floorboard cover that fit perfectly over the dugout and blended with the floor completed Michael's hiding place. For extra concealment, an ancient trunk on wheels—much like a tombstone—would have to be rolled over the hiding place each time Michael was forced to use it, which was any time the Nazi soldiers were present in the village. And that's where I was to come in….

It would be my responsibility to hide Michael safely in his hiding place and roll the aged trunk over the hideout any time I discovered the soldiers were in the village or on the way, which I would be able to spot from the hill in back of our house. I would soon understand what Mother meant when she said, "No child your age should have to be responsible for a job as enormous as I have in mind for you, Luba." But I also understood we were in the midst of a terrible war and this was no time to revel in childhood innocence, even though I was a child. Child or not, I knew what I had to do and what was expected of me. We finally called it a day. And what a day this had been!

"Try to get some sleep—the rooster will crow before we know it," Mother said as she stretched out her tired body on the straw-mattress bed she and I shared topped by a home-made goose-down cover. Mother fell asleep as soon as her head hit the pillow and so did Michael and John and the three of them snored thunderously for the rest of what was left of that night. I tried to sleep, and even made believe I was snoring like the rest of them, but sleep would not come no matter how hard I tried. My tormented mind kept on replaying the events of this unbelievable day and in the process created ones that might or might not come to pass.

Mother had told me earlier that night that if our secret was ever found out by the Nazis that we were hiding Michael from them, the punishment for such a crime could mean death for all of us. Now in the stillness of the sleepless night I imagined every "what if" possibility which could lead the swastika-soldiers to our secret. What if they walked in when I was in the midst of hiding Michael? What if I messed up when I was being questioned about Michael's whereabouts? What if I didn't get home in time to warn Michael? In each case, I begged the soldiers for mercy but was ignored and mocked. And I panicked, while everyone in the house slept peacefully. My job hadn't even begun and I already considered myself a failure—which would bring about our demise. To separate myself from thoughts worse than the worst nightmare, I began to pray for strength and guidance. And God listened to my petition because none of the things I imagined and feared that night came to pass.

Finally the rooster crowed, announcing to the world this dreadful night was officially over. A new day was on the horizon and I was glad to start anew too; to leave behind the thoughts of gloom and doom that were tormenting and poisoning my mind for the last few hours; to make room for thoughts of happy endings and days to come and to revel in them, instead.

The next few days and nights were peaceful, except for a constant stream of war planes whizzing over our heads, polluting the air with deafening noise. I watched in awe and wondered what made those bird-like machines move so quickly through the air, but since they posed us no harm being so far away, I was not afraid of them; rather I was fascinated by them—until this one almost fateful day.

"Luba, I need John to help me around the house today, "Mother said. And I knew this meant I would have my old job of tending the cattle in the pasture fields near the forest back for that day, and she and John would do whatever had to be done and also be on the look-out for the Nazi soldiers. "Michael will be safe, so you need not worry about him," she assured me.

The day was sunny and I welcomed the chance to be free in the fields with nature again. There was still so much to be happy about, in spite of everything that was going on. The colorful wild flowers everywhere; the luscious berries ready for picking; the nearby brook whispering, "Welcome back, Luba! Where have you been? We missed you!" I wished Michael could see what I was seeing. How sad that he couldn't even step outside to see the light of the day, I thought. For now Michael had to live in secret—a secret kept from everyone except Mother, John, and me, I reaffirmed in my mind. I think I'll bring him a bouquet of wild flowers and some berries to cheer him up!

14

Suddenly my reverie was interrupted by a thunderous noise—a noise so deafening that for a split second I thought the world had come to an end as predicted by the village elders. Those humongous planes! They were right over my head—and that's all I remembered. What happened next and why I survived the ordeal that followed, only God knows for certain.

My mother found me as well as our three cows, passed out cold on the ground near where the planes dropped several bombs; for how long the cows and I were passed out, we could only guess. Fortunately, the bombs must have been aimed at the forest, about a quarter to a half mile away from me and the cattle. My mother panicked when I didn't respond to her screams when she found me or even when she shook me with all her might, carried me to a nearby brook, and splashed me with water in an effort to bring me back to life.

"You were limp and lifeless, Luba, and I feared the worst," she later confessed.

Miraculously, I did come back to life (and so did our three cows), slowly and in my own time. Once again I refused to give up on the world even though the world almost gave up on me. Physically I survived the bombs, but the emotional scars from the ordeal would linger on for years to come. But that was a small price to pay compared to what might have been, had I been a little closer to where the bombs were dropped. For certain, one of the several craters—large enough for a decent sized home—created by those bombs, would have become my unfortunate destiny. By the Grace of God I was spared that fate.

My close encounter with bombs made me extremely fearful of all planes. Now I had two enemies to worry about and watch out for: the Nazis and the planes. Every time I saw even a single plane, no matter how high up in the sky, I felt danger and wanted to run for cover. But to keep Michael safe required that I canvass the neighborhood and its surroundings several times a day for Nazis' presence, and running for cover when planes appeared in the sky was not an option for me, no matter how much I feared them.

If I spotted the soldiers, almost always on horseback, galloping down the rolling hills or prancing brazenly through the village, I ran home as fast as my skinny legs could carry me. I looked more like a child of only five or six at that time, I was later told. I would shove Michael into his hiding place, place the cover on top, roll the shabby trunk over the disguised dugout, and nonchalantly play on the floor with whatever was available around the house, mostly pots and pans as I never owned a doll or a toy. The scheme appeared to work for a time. On several occasions the Nazi soldiers came by when I was alone in the house—except for my brother Michael in the hiding place, of course! They took what they found in terms of food and left without paying any attention to me engrossed in child-play. My job turned out to be a piece of cake, I began to think. Luckily, I never trusted the Nazis enough to take my responsibility lightly.

On this day, like any other in the past, I canvassed the neighborhood and at that early hour of the day I found nothing unusual. An hour or so later, I checked again! This time I saw two soldiers in the distance on horseback, heading in the direction of our house. In no time at all I was home, hid Michael in his hiding place, rolled the trunk on top of the hideout and took to my pots and pans on the floor, as usual. Sadly, this visit from the Nazis was different from all others, when all they wanted was something to eat. This time they wanted what was most precious to us—our Michael!

Both soldiers entered the house simultaneously. One sat on top of the trunk over Michael's hiding place, while the other poked around with his rifle. The one atop the trunk asked me to sit on his lap and offered me candy, before he revealed what his mission really was. I took the candy because I wanted him to think I could be bribed and tell him all I knew about Michael's whereabouts. For a brief moment, I thought my heart would stop beating as I feared the worst, but on the outside I forced myself to stay calm and in control of all my senses.

"Is your brother Michael at home?" the soldier asked. I looked him straight in the eyes and as calmly as was possible under the circumstances, I answered.

"Michael doesn't live here any more. And why are you asking me? You should know where he is." I shot back.

"Why should I know?" the soldier asked, puzzled.

"You should know because you took him somewhere a long time ago. And if not you, then someone who looked exactly like you," I told him and even managed to shed a tear or two. The soldier looked surprised and there was a puzzled look on his face. Whether he felt sorry for me—the emaciated child that I was—or believed my story, I will never know, but neither he or the other soldier searched for Michael or questioned me further. After helping themselves to Mother's bread and butter, leaving none for us, they left the house in pursuit of other young victims, while I enjoyed my candy as a reward for a job well done on behalf of us all.

One young victim that day happened to be my brother's best friend, Wasyl, and the other my mother's nephew, John. Both were apprehended and whisked away—to where no one knew. When we were certain the soldiers had left the village, Michael and I held hands and said a silent prayer, thanking God for His blessings. Finally, Michael spoke aloud.

"I'm proud of you, Luba," he said with tears in his eyes. "And to show you how much I appreciate what you've done for me today, I'm gonna teach you a beautiful Lemko song that you and I will sing one day soon, at the top of our lungs and from the top of the highest mountain." And he did! I still remember the words. He then raised a make-believe glass and toasted. "To you, Luba, my guardian angel! To all of us! To the end of this war, to victory and freedom."

But Michael's journey to victory and freedom did not end in his hiding place in our house and with me as his guardian angel. Shortly after the last close encounter with the Nazis, Michael felt his luck was running out. He decided—and Mother agreed—it was time for him to move on and search for another hiding place, "until peace reigns over us once more," she stressed. A place far from home—perhaps a remote farm, where he could work as a hired hand for room and board until the end of the war. Mother gave Michael her blessings and assured him, "I know God will bring you back to us one day. Until that happy moment, remember, our love and our prayers for you are strong enough to outlast any war."

Disguised as an old woman, Michael said a tearful good-bye, and like my father several years earlier, disappeared into the dark night in search of a safer hideout. Sadly, en route to find that remote haven of his dreams, he was apprehended—on a train—by the Gestapo and shipped to Auschwitz Concentration Camp. And if it were not for one solitary postcard Michael managed to send home, we would not have known his whereabouts for another two years when he was liberated at the end of this horrific war. That one blessed postcard from Michael gave us reason to hope.

With Michael gone, the part of me that loved to sing, pick wild flowers, and jump over the bubbling brooks was gone too. I missed my brother more than I ever missed anyone before—even more than my beautiful Star. And still the war raged on. The Nazi soldiers came to the village even more frequently than in the past and there was no pattern to their unwelcome visits. Some days they came early in the morning and some days they came at night; sometime every day and sometime they skipped a few days. And no one knew what damage they would leave behind. Would it be an empty cupboard, a missing horse or cow, or worst of all, a young person now as young as sixteen—like my brother John.

By this time, my brother John became convinced the Nazis were after him each time they showed up in the village. He became obsessed with his eventual capture and upon seeing them in the village one day, he decided to run away from home, leaving no clue of his destination. Mother, stricken with grief, half crazed, went looking for him. She wandered through fields and neighboring villages for several days, in desperate search for John. She even approached Nazi soldiers and questioned them if they had taken her young son, not caring about her own safety. And she told no one before she left on her mission for fear she might be stopped by well-meaning neighbors or family. All of God's angels must have watched over her because on several occasions she came close to being done away with by Nazi soldiers. After all, this was war and she could have been a spy disguised as a grieving mother in search of her child.

This is the way she explained later: "My boy was missing and I had to find him, no matter how high the risks." And the risks were high not only for her but also for me, left at home all alone with all the responsibilities and dangers, at the tender age of ten. The angels that watched over my mother must have watched over me as well, because I managed to stay alive, though confused and frightened, since I wasn't sure I would see my mother or brothers again. Yet, I was afraid to tell anyone about Mother's and John's disappearance. I was used to keeping secrets by now, and thought this one was for keeps, too.

I fed the cows and chickens with what was available in the barn (scraps of hay left over from winter to feed the cows and grain for the hungry chickens). I milked the cows and drank some of the milk. I gathered the eggs, made fires in the wood-stove; and cooked a few eggs for myself to eat each day.

Growing up I listened to many ghost stories shared by young people who met in each other's houses in the evenings during winter months to spin (make threads to be weaved into cloth at a later date) home-grown, prepared flax and entertain themselves by telling ghost stories and jokes. Now that I was by myself in the dark house, I convinced myself ghosts were lurking in every corner. To escape their inevitable wrath, I placed the featherbed next to the wide open door leading to the outside, for a quick escape from a fate worse than death, according to what I had heard about ghosts. Somehow I survived the horror of those nights, but the memories of them haunt me to this day.

After several days, Mother miraculously returned, unharmed, famished, exhausted, and without John. And it was another miracle when Brother John courageously made his way home, after a week or so of hiding in the dense forest, feeding on wild berries, mushrooms, and nuts, and drinking water from the running streams. Luckily, this was summertime—a blessing for us all.

"Will this war ever end?" I heard Mother lament as she and her sister Eugenia talked low so that I wouldn't hear what they were saying. But I heard enough, and what I heard frightened me terribly. Their supposedly secret conversation involved outrageous atrocities the Nazis were committing against the unsuspecting innocent people. Taken from us and not heard from again were hard-working, religious Jewish families, who lived in peace with everybody in the village and were friends of many, including us. Gypsies who bothered no one and lived decent lives shot to death and buried en masse in graves dug by the victims themselves. A man shot to death because he butchered a hog with intentions of using the meat for his own family, which was in violation of the Nazi rule. I was glad I didn't witness any of these atrocities, hearing about them and knowing they really happened—some of them right in our own village—was bad enough.

"What will happen to us? Will any of us survive this ugly war?" Aunt Eugenia sighed.

"I am beginning to think not even God knows the answers to these questions," my mother answered as she kissed her sister good-bye.

But God did know and soon He let His Creation know, too—the lucky ones who had survived this six-year-long war. For them, the sun would shine again and the flowers would bloom, too! The year was 1945! I was twelve years old when this dreadful war finally came to an end!

Chapter 3

Postwar Twists and Turns

The Byzantine-style Church of St. Luke, the spiritual beacon of our village of Liszczyny, was built in the early nineteenth century. It proudly stands atop a hill overlooking the village and its centuries-old cemetery. The church was the center of the spiritual as well as secular life of the villagers. Its chiming bells carried noteworthy messages sent to the faithful—via the wind—to let them know, for example, that someone within the church community had died, especially if the bells tolled at special hours of the day. On Sunday mornings or Holy Days, the bells tolled to summon the faithful to church, and they came in droves. On occasions, the bells tolled when approaching storms, preceded by gathering black clouds and deafening thunder, threatened to destroy the people's livelihood—their precious crops ready for harvest, or their young plants, the promise of a bountiful harvest. How well I remember church grounds crowded with people, some kneeling and some with outstretched hands towards the heavens, all praying the same prayer: "Heavenly, All-powerful Father, save our growing plants/harvest from destruction!" On this day, however, the church bells rang on and off all through the day—a confusing message to the tradition-respecting villagers. Was this a malicious act done by a prankster? A few angry villagers left their field work and trudged to the church to find out. Soon the whole village (and beyond) learned the reason for the tolling church bells on this glorious spring day, May 8, 1945! Shortly, crowds of people gathered around the church to celebrate this long-awaited moment!

They wept tears of joy as they embraced each other. "The war is over—Praise the Lord!" the crowd shouted in unison. "Peace will reign over our land again!" some chimed. "We won the war! We defeated the enemy!" others cried out. I watched and listened in awe and wondered if I should make some noteworthy statement to contribute to this one-of-a-kind event—the end of the war that most people, including me, thought would never end. But I could only think of one thing to add to what was already said:

"Please pray for my brother Michael that he finds his way home from Auschwitz Concentration Camp," I asked, too low for anyone to hear. Then in the same low tone, I added, "and all the others who were taken away, too." My best friend, Pauline, standing next to me, heard my plea and offered to pray with me. She and I had prayed many times in the past for my brother's safe return—and others', too—but this time our prayers were more earnest than ever before. Like it or not, the moment of truth had arrived! Those who survived the Nazi slave labor camps would be coming back; those who hadn't survived would not.

There was nothing in the world I wanted more than for my brother Michael to be among those who were coming back. So when days and weeks passed and spring turned to summer and my brother was still not back, I began to worry, but I never stopped praying and hoping. And when the families of other slave labor victims gave up hope of ever seeing their loved ones again and my mother wept openly for her son—and husband too—I did not weep with her. I prayed instead, and waited patiently for my brother's return. But no matter how hard I tried to get my message of hope to my distraught mother, I couldn't break through the wall of despair that seemed to have closed in on her.

"We have to face facts, Luba, your brother—and father, too—may not be coming back and there is nothing we can do to change that," she would cry out, looking at me through her tear-stained eyes as if the worst that could happen already had.

"I don't know about my father—or others who were taken away—but I do know I will see my brother again," I'd reassure my mother, even though it was clear I was not reaching her. The only person who never doubted my innermost feelings and beliefs in this case was my faithful friend, Pauline.

"I will always stand by you, Luba, for as long as we both shall live," Pauline would tell me, and I in turn would reassure her I would do the same for her—and I meant every word of it. "We will let nothing and nobody come between us and our special friendship. Ever!" We promised each other. And that promise might have withstood the test of time if, our time together was not cut short and our one-of-a-kind friendship physically ended when we were both twelve years old.

Before the war dust fully settled on our Carpathian Mountains and the wary people adjusted to living with their war-ravaged losses, especially their missing loved ones, another blow was about to erupt on their horizon. Less than two months into peace, in the summer of 1945, official-looking men dressed in Sunday-best and speaking eloquent Russian unexpectedly arrived in the village (as well as in other Lemko villages), posing as messengers of good will and good news for all people. At first, the people, barely out of the Nazi clutch, resented the presence of those uninvited individuals in their village. They were exhausted from the long tumultuous years of war and now all they wanted was to be left in peace to work their land and worship their God as their predecessors had throughout the many centuries. But the strangers were adamant about their mission and would not leave the village. Instead, they ingratiated themselves to the unsuspecting peasants and gradually won their trust through coercive means.

Unbeknownst to the people, those official-looking men were members of the Soviet Communist Party who managed to convince about half of the people in our village of Liszczyny, and elsewhere in the Lemko Region, to abandon their ancestral homes in the Carpathian Mountains for a better life and adventure in the Soviet Union. In those days, most country-folks did not travel much beyond the boundaries of their own village, or the neighboring ones so an offer for a better life and adventure in a far-away, magical place sounded exciting—an opportunity of a lifetime. The colorful language similar to their own made the offer even more inviting and appealing.

Our family, Pauline's family, three of my mother's sisters and their families, and one of my father's sisters and her family were among those who allowed themselves to be persuaded to leave their ancestral homes in the Carpathian Mountains and head for the "unknown" in the Soviet Union to live a "life of plenty in the land of honey," as they were promised. At first I rejected the idea that we leave our home. I didn't want to break the connection to our land and home and argued my case. "We're part of this land, the forest, the mountains and the streams that flow through them. If we abandon them, we would be abandoning a part of ourselves as well. And what about Michael? He is coming back, I'll have you know! I want to welcome him home when he walks through that door." I'd insist, pointing to the door.

"Luba, I have reasons to believe your brother will not be coming back," Mother would tearfully say. "I heard from reliable sources that innocent people who found themselves in Nazi concentration camps such as Auschwitz where your brother was shipped to, were burned to death. I already told your brother John about this atrocity but asked him not to tell you until the time was right. Well, it is high time for you to know the truth, no matter how painful. And it is our time to start life anew, away from here and the unpleasant memories which may continue to haunt us unless we leave them behind along with everything else."

I knew that Mother wanted to go where most of her family, some neighbors and friends were going, now that she was convinced she had lost both her son and her husband, so that did not surprise me. What she told me about Auschwitz, where my brother had been a prisoner of war for over two years, not only surprised me, it shocked and devastated me. And although I grieved for all the people who met with such an unbelievable fate at the hands of the Nazis, my young mind didn't fully comprehend the magnitude of it all. So I continued to pray for Michael's safe return and I believed, against all odds, that he was coming back because my prayers were being heard and would be answered. When I shared this insight with my mother she listened, but insisted: "We have to face facts, Luba. Other families prayed too, and still their loved ones in Auschwitz as well as in other camps were tortured and tragically done away with. What makes you so sure

24

Michael was not one of them?" Mother then leaned over and whispered in my ear: "You've been hurt enough, dear child, don't set yourself up for more hurts and disappointments." I realized Mother meant well but I also knew, deep down, I would not be hurt or disappointed. Not this time! I wasn't sure about ever seeing my father, but I had no doubt in my heart about seeing Michael again.

Since half the people in the village were relocating to this "land of plenty" somewhere in the Soviet Union and Pauline was among them, I decided not to question further Mother's decision to go. I put my energy, instead, to helping Mother and John in deciding what to take with us and what to leave behind. I also joined Pauline and other soon-to-be-immigrants in singing a made-up ditty with all my heart and soul. *"Pideme, pideme, juzh tu nebudeme, po Rosijskim poly spivaty budeme."* Translated it meant: "We will go, we will go, we will no longer be here, over the Russian fields we will sing." Where those fields were, no one knew.

We said a quick good-bye to everything we were leaving behind. Mother and Brother John shed a few tears as they closed the door to our house. I felt too numb to cry or feel the sadness of the moment, so I walked away and never looked back. Now homeless, we were on our way to the "promised land" somewhere beyond the horizon. We traveled on foot, with heavy bundles on our backs and livestock by our sides, over the mountain trails to the city of Gorlice, miles away from home. In midsummer heat we were packed into the tight quarters of windowless boxcars together with our livestock, which we led out on a daily basis to water and to graze in the limited grassy areas around the railroad tracks. We followed this routine for as long as we remained stationary—about two weeks as I recall.

Fortunately for our family, just as the freight trains were getting ready to depart a messenger from the village delivered a telegram to us. The timing was unbelievable! "I'm well and pray all of you are well, too. I am anxiously awaiting news from you," the message from my father read. The unexpected good news from my father made our mother re-think her decision. Since our relocation to the Soviet Union was to an unknown destination, Mother became concerned that communication to the outside world might not be possible, so she decided and John and I agreed we should return to our home in the village to await further news from my father and to notify him, via a telegram also, of our situation.

On the return trip to our village, Mother told us why she was convinced we would not see or hear from our father again: "The ship your father had planned on taking back to America had sunk and I was sure he went down with it. I kept this awful secret from you because I wanted to protect you for as long as I could," she confessed. "Your father miraculously must have missed the ill-fated ship and was able to make a safe connection to America via another one," Mother explained with a smile I hadn't seen in a long time. But her smile disappeared as soon as she remembered her elder son was still among the missing.

When I said my tearful good-bye to my best friend Pauline, it did not occur to me I would not see her again, nor any of the other people on the freight train, including my dear relatives. Over the years I wondered how life treated Pauline and if she missed me as much as I missed her, and thought about me as often as I thought about her, even when other friends came into my life. Years later we learned what hardships these unfortunate Lemkos endured as a result of this so-called "voluntary" relocation. And the hardship we were spared because of my father's timely telegram.

When the caravan carrying the homeless Lemkos reached the Soviet soil weeks later—in some instances without an elderly loved one or an infant child not strong enough to survive the rigorous journey—one by one the families were dropped off over the poor post-war Soviet territory. Not all families were given a place to live upon arrival—some remained homeless for a long time. Eventually, our Lemkos accepted their destiny and made the best of what they considered as their lot in life, since most, if not all—for one reason or another—were unable to return to their forsaken ancestral homes in the Carpathian Mountains. By reason of necessity at the time, they settled where they were dropped off—the land known in those days as the Soviet Ukraine—today, independent, free democratic Ukraine! And the once Communist-dominated Soviet Republic, now blessedly-free, God-revering democratic Russia!

Back in our village the empty houses—resembling a ghost town—created an atmosphere of doom and gloom. Life had changed not only for those who left their homes but also for those who chose to remain in their homes. I missed Pauline more than I ever imagined I could miss a friend. Not even the things that once made me deliriously happy made any difference in my life. The birds didn't seem to sing as cheerfully as when Pauline and I heard them together. And the wildflowers didn't seem as vivid as when we admired or picked them together. There was so much sadness everywhere, such emptiness. Even the mountains appeared sad and lonely. When the rains fell upon them and the water cascaded down their slopes, I was sure they were shedding tears for the people who had abandoned them in search of greener mountains.

The days were getting shorter and colder and a blanket of brown hues now lay atop once summer emerald-green grass. Soon a thick cover of snow would conceal the rutted paths leading to our village. "Please God, bring my brother Michael home before the road home is completely obliterated by mountains of snow," I prayed. To appease me, Mother would pray along with me, and even asked Brother John to pray with us. And the three of us prayed earnestly every night for Michael's safe return, until it was time to sleep.

I must have just dozed off when I heard a knock on the window. At first I thought I was dreaming, and when I realized I was awake, I thought hungry Nazi soldiers wanted to be let in to help themselves to some food. Then I remembered the war was over! I jumped out of bed and ran to the window. Mother and John followed in my footsteps and the three of us peeked out through the glass. When we didn't recognize the stranger, we quickly moved away hoping the person on the other side of the window would walk away. But he didn't! Instead, he rapped on the door and refused to give up. Mother lit a kerosene lantern and walked over to the door to ask the stranger a few questions before she let him in. John and I stood next to her in case she needed protection. When she was satisfied he posed no danger to us Mother opened the door, took one look at the stranger in the light and collapsed. The stranger on the other side of the threshold was her son and our brother, Michael. He walked back into our lives the same way he walked out—in the dark of the night.

Michael looked more like a skeleton in the laboratory than an inhabitant of this world. How he had walked hundreds of miles in his condition, begging for food and shelter during the long journey home, I will never know! When Mother finally gained her composure and John and I realized the stranger we feared was no stranger to us, we hugged and kissed Michael until he could take no more. My prayers were answered! Except for missing Pauline, there was joy in my life again. The hues of brown on the autumn mountains suddenly changed to radiant gold to match the color of my spirit.

Shortly after Michael's miraculous return from Auschwitz, other family members—Aunt Eugenia's daughters (Mother's nieces) Anna and Mary, and Aunt Anna's son (Mother's nephew) John—also survivors of Nazi slave labor camps—straggled to our door. Since they found no trace of their families, they turned to ours for help. And we couldn't even tell them the whereabouts of their loved ones, because we didn't know. No one had heard from them. With their families gone God only knew where and their homes empty shells, Mother took them all in. Now our two-room log home was brimming with life once again, especially when Anna and Mary (Nazi rape victims, they claimed) gave birth to their babies—a boy and a girl. Living in such close quarters with two colicky infants became intolerable. Soon, with everyone's cooperation and hard work, Mother's nieces Anna and Mary and their babies, as well as nephew John, moved to their own scantily-furnished but clean homes. Their homesteads left behind by their families.

Life was slowly returning to normal again! Spring of 1946 arrived in full glory, blanketing the hills and valleys with emerald-green velvet grass and multi-colored wildflowers everywhere. The mountains seemed happy again, and the birds sang again, too, but not for everybody. For some people, like the family of my brother Michael's best friend Wasyl, the glorious spring might as well had been a stormy winter. Their only son (at the time) and brother Wasyl did not return. He died with millions of other Nazi victims, and his loved ones had to learn to live without him and bear the pain of not knowing how and where he spent his final hours. To this day I can still visualize Wasyl's father on the first Easter Sunday following Wasyl's demise. He didn't just cry, he wailed, causing the jubilant congregation singing the Resurrection Hymn to shed tears of grief instead of joy, as was customary during the celebration of this Holiest of Days in the Christian calendar.

And there were others, like my brother Michael, Mother's nieces Anna and Mary, and nephew John, who survived this atrocious war but were left with lasting physical and emotional scars. Whose lives would never be the same because the most important parts of their beings—their spirits—were sucked out of them by their bitter experiences while in captivity. However, now that the worst was behind them, the potential for a brighter future in their ancestral homes and surrounding land appeared limitless. The future that was not to be, as we would soon find out.

Chapter 4

Forced Move

The phrase, "you can't judge the book by its cover," brings to mind the Lemko-Rusyn log homes, including the one I lived in. Simple in appearance, yet strong enough to last for generations or even centuries. Built of hand-hewed logs which came from native timber, they represented extensions of members of the same families (in most cases), stemming from the original homestead-owners, onward, families who considered their ancestral homes as sanctuaries to which any of them could always come back to, should the world outside their sturdy walls treat them unkindly. And this was the perception I grew up with regarding my log-home, until the day the unthinkable and unimaginable happened.

When the Second World War finally ended, we truly believed the dark days ended too. Unbeknownst to anyone at the time, this was not to be. In July of 1947—two years after the so called "voluntary move" of 1945 to the Soviet Union—the remaining unsuspecting Lemkos, including our family, faced yet another move. This time it was the forced relocation from their ancestral homes to a destination also unknown—an act so cruel the memory of it will forever haunt me. (For anyone interested in researching this action further, look up "Operation Vistula" or "Akcja Wisla").

The anguish this horrific act created filled me with suppressed anger and rebellion. What other emotions could there be when without warning—true in our case—armed soldiers (this time speaking Polish) appeared at our doorstep and decreed, "You have exactly two hours to round up your livestock, pack your belongings and be ready to leave your home." We pleaded with the soldiers, but soon realized they meant business and all our tears and begging were in vain. We then raced against time to gather as many valuables and heirlooms as we could, and placed everything in burlap sacks to be carried on our backs. Saddened to the brink of desperation, we walked out of our home, followed by the stern-looking, armed soldiers and three restrained cows by our side.

We closed the door to our humble, much loved log home for the last time and with other unfortunate village families headed for the unknown, without a clue as to the reason for this senseless act. Our request to stop at the church before proceeding on to the city of Gorlice beyond the mountains was granted (for our family a deja vu going back to 1945). We knelt at the open church door and thanked God for all the past blessings, while pleading for future ones. We then bade a tearful good-bye to the old church on the hill, the tolling bells gifted by my father in America, and the white washed chapel on the church-grounds, gifted by my grandparents on the paternal side of the family. There were also other displaced families who were desperately praying and weeping with outstretched hands towards the heavens asking God to intervene in this plight. However, God's intervention, in this case, was not revealed to us until many years later, when the history of "Our People" was written and injustice done to the innocent Lemkos was exposed to the world and publicly acknowledged and apologized for by the responsible parties.

However, for all the wrongs done to the Lemkos to be made right again, the words of acknowledgment and apology are not sufficient. They must be followed by actions! Actions speak louder than words, especially in the case of Operation Vistula 1947. We know now that the plight of 1945 and the final blow of 1947—which left our Lemkovyna devoid of people and the land forced to return to wilderness the way it was before it was settled by our predecessors many centuries ago—were politically motivated and agreed upon by the Communist Governments of Poland and the Soviet Union. Both are no longer in existence, except in the history books. Thank God!

To me the windowless boxcar into which we were squeezed with our livestock and meager possessions appeared even more stifling, filthier and harboring more offensive odors than the one I remembered when we found ourselves in the similar situation two years earlier in 1945. But now I was two years older, more sensitive to insensitive treatment at fourteen than at twelve. I was deeply hurt by the way we were treated. On several occasions Mother had to stop me from verbally attacking the soldiers whose orders I was not willing to follow.

"You can't win this battle, Luba, so stop trying. Do as you're told and don't argue. The soldiers are only doing what they were told to do," she would whisper in my ear when no one was looking. And I listened because I knew she was right, even though I didn't agree with her. Secretly I threatened to avenge this violation on our rights. One day the responsible party would pay. No one could take my dignity away from me and get away with it, I vowed.

After two weeks of waiting at the station in scorching July heat, searching for grass and water for our cattle, making-do on the meager food supply we brought with us and the milk from our three cows, the freight trains finally moved on. At the end of another two weeks of the arduous journey—with stops to feed and water our livestock—we arrived in western Poland in a region called Silesia, which until the end of the Second World War had been part of Germany. We knew we had reached our destination when the families in our caravan began to be dropped off one by one—being scattered over the war-ravaged land—miles apart from each other, without as much as an address next to their names.

Our family—along with several other Lemko families from surrounding villages—were dropped off in the fields near a bombed out structure which in its heyday might have been a warehouse. Fortunately, the weather cooperated and there was plenty of good grass all around for our cattle, which supplied us with enough milk to sustain us until we found other sources of food. After the fact, we were told by the earlier settlers there were live land mines still buried in the ground where our cows grazed and how lucky we were not to have stepped on one of them while watching over them. Several days into house hunting, we found a place to live—a house that had its four walls and a roof still intact—a rare find. Most homes around us were bombed-out shells with human skeletons of war victims still in some. To me, this desecrated community we were forced to live in seemed so mysterious and surreal. I never stopped wondering what it might have looked like before the War. What kind of people lived there and what happened to them? In the process of mourning for my home in the mountains, I also remembered the people who called the home we now occupied theirs. Why is life so unfair to some? I questioned.

Once we settled into this shell of a home and thought of our house in the peaceful Carpathian Mountains standing forlorn, the penned-up emotions could no longer be contained. The three of us—Mother, John and I—cried until there were no more tears left. Brother Michael, on the other hand, shed no tears and showed no emotions—good or bad—he just simply looked on. Finally he spoke.

"Pull yourselves together and stop acting as if you've lost everything! True, we were treated unfairly and we lost a lot, but we have our lives and we have each other and that in itself is a precious gift millions of others will never have. Millions of innocent people—including tiny babies and little children—were denied a chance at life and were tortured and then done away with in unimaginable ways. It was only by the Grace of God I was not one of them and only because the war ended and I was liberated before my number came up." Tears like water flowed out of Michael's terrified eyes as he poured out what was, until this moment, too painful to talk about or even cry about. Prior to this time, he kept everything to himself and spoke only when spoken to while gazing into space or out the window of our log home. On one occasion, he ran out of the house in the middle of the night screaming and disappeared in the darkness. We searched for him in the light of the moon and stars until we found him huddled in the corner of the shed, unwilling to speak. We physically carried him into the house. How happy we were that he finally opened up to healing. For the first time we realized what he must have lived through; what suffering and torture he must have endured during the time he was a war prisoner in Auschwitz; not to mention what unspeakable horrors he must have witnessed and then suppressed in order to go on living.

33

Unknowingly, Michael had taught me a valuable lesson. Without a doubt what happened to us was out of the ordinary and unjust but to dwell on it and continue to harbor resentment and thoughts of revenge—most likely against other innocent people—no longer made sense to me. I made up my mind not to think about what we lost but rather what we had left, and with a grateful heart embrace the future and go on from there. We were still among the lucky ones because we had life and we had each other, "and that in itself was a precious gift." Michael taught me that and much more.

I didn't dare complain again—and neither did Mother and John—not in Michael's presence. Although we continued to talk about our forsaken home in the mountains, the maturing plantings with no one to harvest them, and dreamed of the day we would be able to return, Michael didn't appear to be upset. I suppose going back home was his dream too. But our dream was not destined to be, as the years ahead would show.

Unbeknownst to us at the time, we were banned from returning to our homestead in the Carpathian Mountains and that unreasonable ban was not lifted until years later—sometime in the late 1950's early 1960's. Unfortunately, by then most old-timers in exile were gone or too old to start over—The younger generation by then assimilated with no special attachment to the land they were unfamiliar with and not sure they owned. The few who returned had to purchase back the land their parents or grandparents owned, clear it and build upon it from scratch. I proudly commend them for their courage and resilience and wish them Godspeed in their endeavors. To those who will not return (like me) because their lives are now elsewhere, I say: "Let us always remember with reverence the land that gave us our beginnings—the serene and beautiful Carpathian Mountains!"

Slowly we began adjusting to our surroundings and living on the land not of our choosing. To make ends meet, Michael and John were hired out to work for a farming family who had arrived on this terrain before us from eastern Poland and were established farmers. Their pay consisted of enough food to eat and some to take home for Mother and me. On occasions they were given a few coins after the bills were paid and there was money left over. My two brothers worked hard for the farmer but they were treated well and we had enough to eat—that's more than we envisioned. We were lucky! But still we wished we could go home. "This is not our home, we don't belong here," we all agreed.

I found a baby-sitting job and Mother took care of the chores at home. After a few weeks, my baby-sitting job ended and my pay was a baby goat and a tarnished silverware set for six, that the lady I was baby-sitting for found in the ruins of a bombed-out building. I adored my baby goat and wished she could always stay little so I could pamper her and watch her enjoy my attention and give me love in return. Before long my baby goat grew up, but stayed young at heart for as long as I had her, and always enjoyed my pampering as much as I enjoyed showering her with it. That baby goat meant more to me than any amount of money ever could have.

The tarnished silverware set did not impress me at the time. I looked at it once or twice, shoved it to the side and forgot about it. Strangely enough, this set of black forks, knives, spoons, and teaspoons wrapped in tattered brown paper seemed impressed with me and followed me no matter where my life took me. Many years later I decided to clean it. Underneath all the tarnish I found beautifully monogrammed, pure silver pieces that must have belonged to a well-to-do German family who didn't make it alive out of the bombed-out building. How sad! Today—over half a century later—I treasure this beautiful silver cutlery set. When I grace our table with it on special occasions, I feel I am honoring the memory of people who owned it before me. This priceless set is now a conversation piece I am proud to display and tell its story. To me it represents a piece of history which should never be forgotten—for obvious reasons.

When the school opened in September 1947, Mother encouraged me to register. "At least until we're able to go back home," she urged. At fourteen I only had a second grade education. I was able to read and write in Cyrillic, used in Russian and Ukrainian as well as our own Lemko-Rusyn language. In our new sparsely populated village of "Grebocice" the classes were in Polish and limited to five grades only. A problem as to which grade level I would best fit arose. A suggestion was also made that I should not continue with further education. But

Mother would not hear of it. And she handled the situation in the best way she knew how. Even if we were left without milk and butter, she made sure for the rest of the year the principal of the village school and her family had enough. "Trust me, I know what I'm doing," Mother would reassure us, if we questioned her generosity. I was placed in fifth grade and had a friend in a high place, the school principal. I was given a second chance at education because of my mother's foresight.

I worked hard and my efforts paid off. Once I grasped the concept of the new-to-me Polish language I simply took off with it. But still, I never felt as if I belonged. I was homesick and lived for the day when the road for us to go back home to the mountains would open up. "When are we going back?" I would whisper in my mother's ear, so no outsiders would hear I was speaking in my own "Lemko" language which was frowned upon by some who didn't understand. One sad day instead of learning a new lesson in class, we learned a bitter lesson of life. We attended a funeral of a classmate—an only child in the family—who lost his life when he stepped on a live mine while playing in his back yard. This tragedy sent a clear message to us in school and at home that the perils of war did not end when the war ended. They would continue to haunt us for years to come.

I completed fifth grade successfully and with honors. And because of my high marks (and maybe the milk and butter supplied to the school principal?), it was recommended that I skip the sixth grade altogether and register for seventh grade in the city of Glogow, about ten or twelve kilometers from home. I was flattered but not happy about the recommendation. What I really wanted was to go back home to the mountains and reclaim what I still believed belonged to us. I was wrong—perhaps because the whole truth was not revealed to us until much later.

"As long as we're still here and you're doing so well in school, you might as well continue," Mother urged. I thought about it and took her advice because she almost always knew what was best for me.

I wanted to hop right back on my bicycle and peddle as fast as I could out of that God-forsaken place. What must have been a beautiful German city, called Glogau before the war, was now a rubble of cement.

A mass grave for the unfortunates who happened to be in the wrong place at the wrong time. And I didn't want any part of this morbidity. The village where we now lived (Grebocice) was bad, but didn't compare to what I saw in the city where I was to continue my education.

"How can I concentrate and learn anything in an atmosphere that reeks with anguish, suffering and death—a city that will forever grieve for those entombed in its ruins?" I protested. "And what is the point to studying when there is no guarantee that such senseless destruction will not be repeated in my lifetime?" I questioned Mother and anyone who would listen.

"More reasons why you should study and learn as much as you can," I heard Mother say. "I cannot guarantee that this will never happen again. Nor can I explain why it happened. Why some people survived and others met violent and untimely deaths. But I know one thing for sure. It would be wrong to give up on life and opportunities because other lives were senselessly destroyed," Mother gently lectured. Was I doing that—giving up on life and opportunities by not wanting to continue my schooling among the ruins? Mother's simple psychology left me with lots to think about and even more to ponder.

The commute to and from school was long and difficult. Pedaling my brother's dilapidated man's bicycle back and forth exhausted me much too much. Some days I came to school soaked to the bone with hardly any strength left for the busy day ahead. But somehow I persevered. Once I acquired the taste for learning I wanted to learn more. I realized how much I had missed during the war years when there was no school. And I became determined to catch up on lost time while the opportunity was there. Finally, my mother's advice made sense.

In time the destruction all around me, school building sheared in half and the remaining half where the classes were held riddled with shrapnel holes, became part of the normal scene and ceased to bother me so much. My preoccupation with returning to the mountains gave way to learning about things outside and in addition to my beloved mountain home. But I will never forget it and one day I will return, I vowed.

When days became short and snow covered the way to school, my means of transportation—the ancient bicycle—became inadequate.

To continue with my education in the City, I needed a place to live closer to school. A family—father and two daughters—agreed to let me share the girls' room as well as their simple meals, in exchange for firewood, and milk products my family supplied; also used clothing my father sent from America. The barter system worked and I was able to stay in school through the winter months.

At fifteen I thought about boys but I had no particular one in mind. One day, a boy in my class named Peter looked at me in the way no other boy did before. Peter was smart, cute, even-tempered and looked up to in class. I enjoyed his special attention and glances and encouraged him by returning the same in his direction. Our mutual admiration for each other grew with time and I couldn't have been happier. I was falling in love with Peter—my first love. The feeling so special that only first love, I found out as I got older, could claim for its own. And I planned to nurture this precious gift of love in the deepest part of my heart where it could grow and bloom for all seasons of my life. But this was not to be. My destiny had plans of her own and no regard for mine.

The news I received from my mother when I came home from school for the weekend in April, 1949, put me in an emotional spin. It would change my life forever. Mother told me, "Your father wants you to go to America," and handed me a letter from him to read and some official-looking documents to look over. I vehemently protested. "It's a bad idea and I will not go," I told Mother. To my astonishment, Mother appeared to be in favor of my father's wishes.

Emigrating to America without my mother and brothers, to live with a father I didn't know, was the last thing I wanted to do. If anything, I eventually wanted to go back to the mountains. But for now, I enjoyed basking in my newly found successes—school and first love.

Unfortunately, the decision to go or not to go to America was not mine to make. I was taught from early childhood parents were to be honored and obeyed. This kind of indoctrination led me to believe I had to listen to my mother and father, even though I didn't agree with them. They knew what was best for me and acted in my best interest and out of love for me, I had to believe. And since my father found a way to get me to America because I was still a minor, it was in my best interest to take advantage of this golden opportunity, my family told me. After all, America is the land of great opportunity and the best place in the world to live in, they insisted, even though none of them had ever been there.

Regretfully and sadly, I said good-bye to my friends in school and to Peter. And on May 12, 1949, two days after my 16th birthday my mother and brothers took me to the airport in Warsaw, to help me carry my two tattered suitcases, packed with things that belonged to me, including my shattered dreams.

Chapter 5

The Farewell

The dreaded farewell moment had arrived! This was the place, the airport in the capital city of Poland, Warsaw, where I had to say good-bye to my family. Perhaps never to see them again, or at best, years from now. The reality of the moment struck me like a ton of bricks literally. I felt as though my very being suddenly split into two parts. One part of me pleaded to forget about America and go back home with my mother and brothers on the same train that brought me here. The other part echoed from afar: "I am your father and I want to be a part of your life. Don't disappoint me, Luba!" Was it too late to change my mind? Was my fate sealed forever? These questions tumbled in my mind like waves on a stormy ocean I was about to fly over.

"Luba, it's time to go!" I faintly heard my mother say as she whispered in my ear, tears streaming down her cheeks. "This is a cloudy day for you and for us, too. But the sun will come out again—it always does. Until then you must make your own sunshine—and we must also. God bless you, my child!"

At that moment, I realized going back home with my loved ones was no longer an option. My destiny was clearly pointing in the direction of America—sadly, it did not include my mother and brothers. For better or for worse, I must journey on, alone.

"Don't ever give up! Always look on the bright side! When things get tough you get even tougher! Instead of crying, smile!" Brother Michael said while we hugged and kissed good-bye. Brother John, on the other hand, could only whisper, "I love you, little sister," and turned away from me. Was he hiding tears? I couldn't tell because my eyes were flooded with tears of my own.

Stunned, I found myself on the other side of the gate which separated me from my family. For a moment I stood motionless, confused and frightened. Again, the thought of going home with my family resurfaced. I felt trapped when the gate would not open to the side where they stood, frantically waving and throwing kisses in my direction. I had no choice but to move forward with the rest of the passengers. But I walked backwards for as long as I was able to see the tiniest specks of my family in the distance. Much too soon they disappeared from my view and I must have disappeared from theirs.

Never before had I seen an airplane close up. Ever since the war planes dropped bombs in the forest near the pasture fields where I kept watch over our grazing cows, I had been deathly afraid of all airplanes. During the war years, when we saw planes flying low we ran for cover whenever possible. At night we covered our windows with black shades so no light—no matter how faint—could be seen from our kerosene lamp (there was no electricity) to make us vulnerable for bombing. Now I was at the entrance of this monstrous machine that would fly the same sky as the enemy planes flew then, and I was at its mercy to carry me over the vast ocean to America.

I climbed the steps to the airplane and stopped at the open door, holding my documents in one hand and a small carry-all bag in the other. Frightened, I wondered where I should go from there. Which seat should I take in the rows of identical ones in front of me? I was relieved when a young woman, dressed in a navy blue two-piece suit and a skimpy hat, directed me to my seat—at least I was spared that decision. I was also relieved that my seat happened to be by a window, so I could bury my tear-stained face in the corner and not have to look at anyone. I didn't know how to fasten my seat belt so the nice young woman in the blue suit (the stewardess, I learned later) showed me how. With everyone safely buckled in their assigned seats, followed by a brief demonstration of the safety equipment in case of an emergency, we appeared ready for takeoff! Once again the reality of the moment filled me with apprehension, sadness, and desire for my safe-haven log home of the past, and the two trusty oak trees in back of it, where Pauline and I spent many precious hours of our child-hood, decorating the make-believe house with wildflowers of every season. After a brief time on the runway, the plane nosed up. Soon we were high above the ground and then in the white, fluffy clouds. From time to time, I glanced at the disappearing land below, while drying the salty tears cascading down my cheeks like streams from the moun-tains when winter snows change to water in spring.

Gliding over what appeared like an endless ocean, a scene from long ago came to mind that seemed to parallel my own life at that moment in time. One sunny spring day as Pauline and I played house in our usual place under the oak trees, a baby bird, fully feathered but still unable to fly, fell from its nest and landed in our play area. We gently picked it up and placed the fledgling in a nearby bush. His par-ents screeched at the top of their lungs to scare away any predators, including us. We slowly moved away and watched from afar as father bird fed the baby bird earthworms and hovered over him until he felt his little one was strong enough to fend for himself. Mother bird, meanwhile, flew back to the nest to tend to the rest of the babies. I felt like that young bird that left the nest too soon. Dressed in grown-up clothes, I might have appeared ready to take on the new world, but on the inside there was still a child in need of parental guidance, espe-cially since I didn't know any English and would be living with a father I did not remember.

The billowing white clouds outside my window slowly disap-peared as approaching night ushered in darkness. The same pleasant stewardess who directed me to my seat brought me a tray of fancy looking food. I examined it but couldn't swallow any of it even though I made several attempts—I was too distraught to eat dinner. I might have taken a bite or two from the huge orange the stewardess brought me later on in the evening, but I didn't know how to peel the thing. Upon further examination (this was the first time I had seen a real orange), I decided the orange was too beautiful to eat, anyway. I care-fully wrapped it in a napkin and put it in my carry-all bag to bring to my father as a present, in addition to the dried mushrooms from our own forest back home that I was bringing him. During the twelve-hour flight the only nourishment I took was a glass of water.

My mind was preoccupied with other important concerns, and food was not one of them.

My perplexed mind refused to let my tense body relax even for a few winks of sleep. While the plane glided over and above the billowing white clouds, I chastised my foolish pride for holding me back from telling Peter how special he was to me. Now he would never know. I questioned myself why didn't I give him my address in America and ask for his in return so we would be able to correspond with each other? How different my life might have turned out if I did that. But I didn't, and now it was too late. If I had a second chance I would do things differently, I was sure. Unfortunately, some things in life—like first love—come but once. I had my chance and let it slip away. I felt so bad and so sad. I thought about Pauline and how different our lives would be. We'll be living in the opposite corners of the world and probably never see each other again, or even exchange letters, since neither of us knew of each others' whereabouts.

Towards the morning my thoughts turned closer to my new home—to the father I was about to meet. I wondered if he looked anything like the picture I had of him in my carry-all bag, the picture that was always in the drawer by the bed my mother and I shared when I was a child living in our log home. And if anyone asked me where my father lived, I would yank the drawer open and point to the picture. "He lives in the drawer, don't you know?" I would proudly announce and wondered why that bright statement from my lips never failed to bring lots of laughs.

I wondered about the house my father lived in. Will there be flowers and grass around it? Flowers, grass under my feet, and singing birds always made me very happy. I wondered if my family felt as sad going back home without me as I felt journeying to America without them. Would I ever again meet someone as special as Peter, or a friend as faithful as Pauline? And how would I be able to communicate with anyone in America when I didn't know one word of English? "Dear God, what have I gotten myself into," I sighed.

Early dawn light began to filter through the ocean of darkness outside my window, changing the sky to gray, blue-green, and finally to pink before the grand entrance of the orange-red sun. Soon there was sunshine everywhere—the same sun I left behind was now gracing the world with its life-giving light on this side of the ocean too—a comforting thought flashed through my mind. The end of my long journey and beginning of my new life was about to begin. I knew I was approaching my destination because in the distance I spotted land and an endless stretch of tall buildings that seemed to reach up to the sky, like some giant evergreen trees in our forest back home.

From an overhead speaker an announcement came and I understood what I needed to know—Idlewild Airport, New York. I was in America! The sadness and fear of the unknown that almost consumed me began to slowly subside—the worst was over. I was now in this "foreign" land, and yet I was still under the same sky I left behind. Shortly, I would be walking the same earth, breathing the same air and enjoying the same sunshine as I did back home. This connection between "over there" where my loved ones were and "over here" where my father was made me feel much more at ease, because I knew it was as much of eternal nature as was our love for each other. I was ready and anxious to meet my new father.

I washed my puffy eyes and tear-stained face, combed my tangled blond hair and applied a little color to my pale cheeks and lips. At home Mother was against me using makeup, but I was sure she would understand this was a special occasion—May 14, 1949—when I arrived in America. Looking good on the outside made me feel better on the inside, too. I smiled again and it felt good when people around me smiled back. And that's how I would greet my father—with a smile—and maybe a hug, too, I decided.

Chapter 6

My New Home

Even though we had not exchanged any words during the long overseas airplane trip to America, on some personal level I felt a sense of camaraderie towards the person in the next seat and the people sitting across the isle from me. Upon leaving the plane, I instinctively walked close to my traveling neighbors, feeling safe in their presence and confident they would lead me to where my father would be waiting for me.

When my traveling neighbors stopped, I stopped right behind them. And when I saw them retrieving their luggage, I scanned the area for mine and retrieved it too, making sure I did not lose sight of their familiar faces. With suitcases in both hands, I hurried to catch up to my one-sided friends. Eventually we all reached the United States Customs Bureau. I stood in line behind them and watched with an eagle eye their every move. I became frightened when my self-imposed friends passed their customs inspections gathered their scattered belongings from the counter, closed the suitcases, and scurried away. I sadly watched them disappear from my view—much like my family back at the airport in Warsaw some twelve hours earlier. Once again I felt alone and confused. Could I find the way to my father on my own? I began to pray silently for guidance.

I watched in disbelief when the items from my suitcases were dumped and scattered over the counter—my personal things rummaged through with no regard for my feelings and sense of privacy. And when the strings of dried mushrooms I was bringing to my father for a present were set aside, I could no longer hold back the tears. I reached over to retrieve my "treasures," but the customs officer pushed back my hand, and pointed to a sign. Of course, I couldn't read what he obviously wanted me to know, but it was clear my father would not be getting the special gift of dried mushrooms from me. My "treasures" were confiscated; no food items or plants of any kind were allowed to cross the United States borders, I found out later. I was glad I still had the beautiful orange I had received on the plane—now the one and only present to give to my father.

I crammed my disheveled things into the two suitcases and, on the spur of the moment, decided to wait for the people behind me, next in line for inspection. I now prayed they'd be the ones to lead me to the waiting area where I would meet my father. I knew when we reached that place because I recognized my other traveling neighbors from the plane, the ones who became lost to me following the customs inspection. I found an empty seat close to them and that's where I settled for the time being.

Soon the people I trusted to get me to this point began to disperse, one by one. I watched as their loved ones greeted them with bouquets of flowers, tears of joy, hugs and kisses, and then walked away with them. I felt a twinge of sadness and loss because unbeknownst to my traveling neighbors—and beyond my understanding—I felt connected to them. I became concerned when the last person from the plane left the waiting area and my father still hadn't shown up. Or was he there but we didn't recognize each other? A thought flashed through my mind which upset me further.

Up to this moment I had worried about the way I would greet my father when we met. What words should I use and how emotional should I get so as not to embarrass him and myself or appear too overbearing or too indifferent? When an hour had passed and no sign of my father, a worry of another kind surfaced. What on earth would I do if my father never showed up? Who could I turn to for help when I didn't speak one word of English or know anyone to call upon? Was I in trouble? If so, I questioned myself how should I handle my problem? After some thought, I decided my situation was neither problematic nor an emergency—not yet. It only meant that I would have to wait a few minutes longer for my father, I reassured myself. As I continued to wait, my mind turned to things in my immediate surroundings.

I realized this enormously large and crowded Idlewild Airport on the outskirts of New York City was the largest, busiest, and noisiest single room I had ever seen or even imagined. It overwhelmed me and reminded me of an outdoor marketplace I once saw where people— like busy ants in the middle of a castle construction—rushed around in pursuit of bargains; meanwhile, anxious-to-sell merchants hollered colorful phrases to attract buyers to their wares.

To make me less anxious while I continued to wait, now well beyond the reasonable time, I indulged myself in thoughts of happier times—experiences of my long-gone childhood. Instead of the huge indifferent airport with intimidating glaring bright lights from the overhead fixtures, loudspeaker announcements in a language I didn't understand, and strangers hurrying in all different directions, I chose to see: A fenced-in meadow in spring where a profusion of vibrant wildflowers nonchalantly sway in gentle breezes. Birds, warmed by the smiling sun, chirping in budding trees while building nests for the next generation of their species. Soon reality interrupted my reverie. I'd been waiting for my father in this God-forsaken place for two hours. I was hungry, penniless, alone—and if my father didn't come for me soon or not at all—homeless too. Please God lead my father to me or show me the way to him, I began to pray—first silently and then out loud.

When another half-hour had passed and still my father hadn't shown up, I could no longer tolerate the situation of not knowing. This was now an emergency! It was time to act! I removed my father's picture from my carry-all bag, took another good look at it and decided to search for him myself. I hadn't gotten very far from where I had been waiting for almost three hours when I spotted a short, thin man, wearing a hat and glasses—a spitting image of my father in the picture and how I perceived him in my mind. He was walking with another man and a policeman. My spirit soared because I thought I had finally found him, but it quickly plummeted when the man I thought was my father looked at me and didn't stop. I was wrong and felt disappointed. "What should I do now?" I whispered to no one in particular. *Run after the man! Don't let him get away*, a voice from nowhere seemed to say. Don't second guess your self. Act!

I moved as quickly as I could through the crowd, dragging my two suitcases behind me, eyes glued on the three men ahead of me, especially the one wearing the hat. When I caught up to the trio, I tapped the man I thought might be my father on the shoulder, and prayed I wasn't making a mistake.

"I'm Luba, would you by any chance be...?" And before I finished the sentence, the man in the hat picked me up, squeezed me as hard as he could, and without uttering a word, began twirling me around with such strength that for a moment I thought I would lose my breath. I knew I had finally found my father! My prayers were answered! But then in the middle of our jubilation, something unexpected happened that caused my old fears to return. The accompanying policeman interrupted our emotional reunion and ordered my father to the side for questioning. Silently I questioned what could have gone so wrong when everything seemed so right only moments earlier? I was further perplexed when the policeman asked for my documents. I had already gone through the customs and was cleared, so why did the policeman want my documents? Reluctantly I handed the documents over to him, imagining myself in big trouble—even deportation! A day or so earlier, I would have been glad to be in this situation—going back home to my family was my wish. Now that I was here and had met my father, I wanted to see for myself what was so great about America and also experience the joy of having a father to call my own.

I felt relieved when the policeman returned my documents, patted me on the shoulder, shook my father's hand, and walked away. Again, my father picked me up and with tears trickling from under the frames of his thick glasses, began twirling me around until I felt dizzy. When he finally let go of me, it was my turn to tell him how I felt about meeting him. But what could I say or do to top or even come close to my father's overzealous reception? Or should I even try? I decided to say only what was in my heart. Looking him in the eyes, I gave him a quick peck on his cheek and told him:

"I'm glad you're my father and I hope you will always be glad I'm your daughter." The few simple words I managed to say to him caused another flood of tears. My father just couldn't stop crying, but there was no doubt in my mind he was extremely happy and the tears he shed were tears of joy. My father welcomed me to America with overwhelming enthusiasm. I wished I could have greeted him with similar emotions, but if I had, I would not have been true to myself nor him. Deep down, however, I knew one day I would love him as much as he had loved me all along. In his case, time and distance were not powerful enough to stifle his love for me or for the rest of his family. Sadly, in my case, time and distance made all the difference, because the opportunity to develop true love for my father was not there.

"Luba, before we begin our trip home I need to explain something," my father said as he motioned for me to sit next to him on the bench in the waiting area of the airport. I wondered what was so important that needed to be explained right this minute. I felt weak from all the emotions, hungry from not eating for a long time, and tired from a sleepless night on the plane. But my father seemed adamant about something he had to explain, so I let go of my own needs and focused my attention on his.

"First let me introduce you to my friend," he said. (The other man I saw walking with my father and the policeman). "Harry is the driver who will take us home. You see, I have no car and I don't drive," my father confessed and continued as he nervously shifted from side to side on the bench next to me.

"While driving to the airport to pick you up, Harry changed lanes and passed up several cars in the Holland Tunnel. He didn't know, and neither did I, that changing lanes and passing traffic in a tunnel is prohibited. We were picked up by the police and received a hefty ticket. According to the police, we could have caused one or several serious accidents, and we were detained for an hour or so to answer questions regarding driving laws. We then arrived at the airport much too late. In my desperation and haste, I chose the wrong gate of your arrival." He paused, took off his glasses, dried his moist eyes with a snow-white handkerchief he took out of his pocket, and went on:

"A young girl your age came by and I felt positive she was you, Luba. In my excitement and joy I didn't bother to ask for her name to be sure. Like a fool, I picked her up, squeezed her tight and swung her around a few times. I even dared to hug and kiss her. The girl, frightened to death (and who could blame her) began to scream. I realized, too late, I made a big mistake. The police came and for a while I was in a lot of trouble and had to answer questions which caused another hour or so of delay. And then there was the wrong gate of your arrival and the reason for the policeman as my escort to prove my innocence." He fidgeted a little, took off his glasses, cleaned them again and went on:

"I hope you can understand why you had to wait for me as long as you did before I showed up or rather before you found me. I ask for your forgiveness." When my father finally finished his story, I noticed he was crying again and his hands were shaking. I took off his glasses and with a handkerchief of mine, I dried the tears from his red eyes, took his trembling hands in mine and told him:

"Of course, I understand and as far as forgiveness, there is nothing to forgive," I assured him, even though I had no idea what "changing lanes" and "passing up traffic in a tunnel" or "getting a hefty ticket" meant. At home I was not exposed to tunnels and cars so I couldn't relate to the problem. But I certainly could relate and understand the predicament my father put that young girl in, because he mistook her for me; how frightened she must have been when a stranger rushed up to her, squeezed, twirled, and hugged her with all his might. I understood, because I experienced the same. However, in my case, he did it for the right reason.

Now that everything was in the open and there were no hard feelings between my father and me, I decided the time was right to ask him to get me something to eat before I passed out and caused a scene of my own. He offered to treat me and Harry to something very special which also happened to be his favorite food, "but first we will pack your things into the trunk of Harry's car and drive around a little to a place that serves this specialty," he informed. I wondered what my father's favorite food would taste like as I smacked my lips in anticipation. By this time, I was convinced I could eat anything that resembled food. But could I really?

50

Driving on busy New York City streets I watched in awe—much like a toddler seeing things for the first time—the towering buildings appearing and disappearing before us. "These tall buildings are called skyscrapers," my father said, pointing to ones in front and on the sides of us. I marveled how such tall buildings could stand up and not topple over when hurricane winds rumbled around them, much like they did, at times, in our own Carpathian Mountains, uprooting some giant trees in their paths. I wished we could stop so I could take a better look at those skyscrapers from a standing position on the ground; to see how high into the sky they actually reached. But I was glad when I heard my father ask Harry, "See if you can find a place to park the car."

After turning a few corners, Harry found a space to squeeze his car into. I was amazed at the precision with which he maneuvered such a huge automobile into such a small space. I was also amazed at all the cars there were in New York City. I figured the people in America had to be very rich to afford so many cars; and also very smart to have built such huge buildings. I wondered if my father was rich, too. And if he lived in a similar skyscraper. Where I came from only a select few could afford a car; in the mountains at the time, no one owned a car that I knew of, and the highest building I had ever seen was a three or four-level structure in the city.

With Harry's car safely in place, we began walking. I felt intimidated by the speeding cars on the crowded streets and hurrying, oblivious people we had to dodge on the sidewalks, so I chose to stay between my father and Harry for safety reasons. To me this first walk in America might as well have been a walk on the moon, Jupiter, or Mars—a world so different from the one I left behind that I felt completely astounded by it. When I looked up at the skyscrapers my head spun and I wondered how the people who lived and worked in them felt. I was glad I had my feet firmly planted on solid ground for now.

I became fascinated by all the pushcarts stationed on the sidewalk and all they had to offer to the curious onlooker like me. At one point I almost asked my father to buy me a small *kielbasa* with sauerkraut (hot dog with kraut) because the sight of it and the savory smell reminded me of home, or a bag of roasted chestnuts whose aroma brought back memories of potatoes roasting on an open fire in the fields at harvest time, or a golden brown salted pretzel and hard candy which reminded me of the treats Mother brought home from her trips to the marketplace in the city.

On the morning of the planned trip to the market, Mother would get up at dawn, pack all the eggs our chickens had laid in the past few days (two or three dozen), butter and cheese we made from the milk our three cows supplied (two or three pounds of each), and on her back she would carry her treasures over the mountains to the marketplace in the city of Gorlice, miles away from home, to sell. For the money she raised, she would buy household amenities, such as sugar, salt, matches, kerosene…. And if she still had money left over—and she almost always made sure she did—a pretzel and a few pieces of hard candy for me and a *kielbasa* or two for my brothers. I could hardly wait for my mother to come home from the marketplace, because the mere thought of the salted pretzel and the candy, made my mouth water. Now the wafting aroma of the foods in the pushcarts made these memories come alive and made my mouth water once again. I felt ravenous, but decided to save my appetite for the special dish my father promised.

Soon we found a restaurant with walls solely dedicated to pictures of different creatures of the sea, and a wide smile appeared on my father's face. I figured this was the place where I would eat my first meal in America and my taste buds could hardly wait. When the plate of strange food was placed before me I felt disappointed. I was very hungry, but could I swallow something so slimy and shimmery that still looked alive, or a red thing with claws and strings protruding from its shell-like body?

"Clams on half-shell—they're fresh from the ocean and still kicking—and live lobsters boiled only minutes ago. Enjoy!" my father said. That's all I had to hear—creatures from the ocean "still kicking" and lobsters boiled alive. How on earth could I bite into a living thing? Or break the shell of another, boiled alive because of me? There seemed to be no rhyme or reason for this atrocious act! I thought, and even questioned my father's professed love for me. If my father knew anything about me, he would know I could never eat such outrageous food as raw clams or lobster encased in its shell and, worst of all, cooked while still alive. I realized my father and I were complete strangers to each other. I knew nothing about him and he knew nothing about me—I thought—as I stared at the untouched plate of raw clams and boiled-alive lobster in front of me, topped with lemon pieces, another food I had not tasted before and had no intention of doing so any time soon.

Only once or twice in my life did I eat fish, and it was a trout one of my brothers caught with his bare hands in the shallow river (reduced to a stream during occasional droughts,) that flowed in back of our log home; I ate it well cooked and smothered with butter. That was all the exposure I had to bodies of water and fish. In spite of the absence of fish in our river most of the time, I loved playing there when I was growing up. Skipping over the rocks with my best friend Pauline, and getting to the other side of the river atop rocks without falling in the water, was one of our favorite games to play on hot summer days.

Watching my father and Harry eating those poor sea creatures with gusto made me sick to my stomach and nauseous. When they were almost through devouring them, and my portion remained untouched, I mustered enough courage to speak out:

"I am not feeling so well and I don't feel like eating—I am sorry," I told my father—not the whole truth but close enough, I thought. He looked up at me, nonchalantly picked up my untouched plate and placed it between Harry and himself. While drizzling lemon over the clams, he said:

"We'll be home soon! There'll be plenty of fruit and other light things for you to eat that will probably sit better on your stomach than clams and lobster. There'll be plenty of other occasions to enjoy such foods," he reassured me, while digging into a humongous plate of raw clams and boiled-alive lobster, and motioning to Harry to do the same. Never will I eat such stuff! I thought. And I chastised myself for not telling my father the truth about his favorite food. Why didn't I tell him the real reason for my sickness? If he knew the sight of clams and lobsters was the culprit that caused me pain, he would most likely treat me to a delicious hot dog, topped by lots of sauerkraut, a salted huge pretzel, and maybe even a few pieces of candy. We were sure to see them displayed in the pushcarts on the way back to the car. I resolved that from now on I would stay away from half truths and stick to whole truths only. Even if the truth hurts, I would always be honest with my father! I silently vowed.

On the way to my new home via the Holland Tunnel, my father proudly announced: "This amazing tunnel was built in 1927, and I clearly remember when it was under construction. It is completely under water! Can you imagine that? The Hudson River is flowing right over it! You'll be living in Jersey City, and our apartment happens to be only a couple of blocks from the Hudson River; a few minutes by car once we leave the Tunnel." As much as I wanted to hear more about this wondrous structure under water, I was glad to know we were almost home. I was anxious to see what my father's place—my new home—looked like, and I was famished and tired.

We passed several empty lots and rows upon rows of two, three, four, and a few five-level brownstone buildings before we reached the street my father lived on. Surprisingly his block was closed off to traffic and crowded with people of all ages, especially children and young adults. Everyone seemed overwhelmingly happy—some were even dancing in the street to music I was not familiar with. However, the rhythmic beat of the drums was unmistakably of international flavor and pleasant to my ears. Finally, my father remembered. "The new mayor was just elected and this is the block party in his honor," he explained. "The music and the noise will probably last well into the night," he warned, looking in my direction.

"I won't mind even if the music and the noise last all night," I assured him. My father laughed and added: "Consider this your party then, Luba, and enjoy—your special welcome to America!" I was touched, even though the celebration on our street had nothing to do with me but by coincidence was very timely, which left me with a pleasant and lasting memory.

"How about something to eat and drink—it's all on the mayor, you know," my father joked. There were hot dogs, pretzels, lots of soda and candy and other foodstuffs I was not familiar with.

"Yes! I would love a hot dog with lots of sauerkraut and maybe a pretzel and a drink—please." I was too embarrassed to ask for some candy, too. My father and Harry brought back a whole bunch of hot dogs topped with sauerkraut, several drinks, and a few golden-brown salted pretzels. We ate standing up but we all enjoyed this unexpected feast, especially me. My first meal in America was just what I wished for. When we finished eating, we picked up my suitcases from the trunk of Harry's car and thanked him for his kindness. While saying good-bye, my father slipped some money into Harry's hand, and he and I walked side by side, to our apartment.

We stopped in front of a row of weather-beaten attached brownstone buildings with rusted steps running down their sides—fire escapes, I learned later. My father pointed to one of the buildings and proudly announced. "This is where you'll be living, Luba! How do you like it?"

I smiled politely, nodded my head but said nothing. To answer that question honestly, I needed to see much more than the outside of an old building. I needed to see the place on the inside. The garden— I was sure there was one—where spring flowers bloomed. And the orchard where fruit trees were laden with white and pink blossoms. After all, this was May, the month when all nature awakens from a long winter sleep, takes on colorful garments and flaunts itself on the world. This was my world back home in the mountains, and I expected nothing less in America—the Land of Plenty!

My father opened the door, right off the sidewalk, to a hallway permeated with a strange odor.

"Garbage day today. I guess it wasn't picked up, yet," he said apologetically, when he noticed my crinkled-up nose because of the foul smell. We climbed three flights of semi-dark winding stairs lit by one light bulb on each landing and no windows. Was this an indication of what my father's apartment—my new home—will look like? I wondered! He opened the door.

"Welcome to your new home, Luba!" he proclaimed with a broad smile.

My new home was a small three-room apartment with a bathroom. The first room off the hallway was the kitchen. Two windows in the kitchen let in enough sunlight to make the room seem cheerful—but not what I expected. One window, enhanced by a small table and two chairs, overlooked a rooftop of another apartment. The other window, facing the street, overlooked an onion-domed church, several three-level apartment buildings to the right and a soap factory to the left. A three-door dish cabinet hung on the wall above the sink in the space between the two windows in the kitchen. A gas stove and a kerosene heater rested against the bathroom wall. And there were two bedrooms off the kitchen to the left, each barely big enough to fit a single bed and a small dresser. And yes, there was a tiny window in each bedroom and a clothes closet, too.

The bathroom with a bathtub and hot water seemed to be my father's pride and joy. "Most places around here have them in hallways and without a bathtub and hot water, and it is shared by all the families living on that floor; I'll have you know," he stressed. I was impressed, considered the indoor plumbing a luxury and told him so. Especially when I recalled the harsh winter nights when I had to leave the warm bed to find my way to the outhouse in the dark. Bathrooms back home in the mountains were outhouses built away from the living quarters, usually near the barns and chicken coops. The place I lived in last had an indoor bathroom, but in a separate part of the house and with no running water—not a pretty sight.

"Luba, this will be your room." My father pointed to the second bedroom off the kitchen. "The furniture in it belongs to my roommate, who will move everything to his new apartment across the hall later on today. It will take a few days before your bed and dresser will be delivered. I'm afraid you'll have to sleep on the floor until then—I hope you won't mind," my father said apologetically, once again, and added, "but I do have the fluffiest featherbed you've ever seen, for you to sleep on until then."

Before long there was a knock on the door. My father's former roommate came to move his bed and dresser to an identical apartment, across from ours, which he would share with another man in same situation as my father was prior to my arrival. I cleaned my tiny room as best I could, placed the featherbed on the floor and was ready to call it a day. I said good night to my father and closed the door behind me. In the morning I would look for the garden and the blooming trees.

56

Chapter 7

Blossoms of Inspiration

I plunged into the featherbed, closed my eyes and must have lapsed into an immediate deep sleep. A few hours later—long before dawn— half asleep and disoriented, I sprang up. *Where am I?*

"You're in America! Don't you remember your father boasting about the fluffy featherbed last night, the one you're now sitting on? Remember...! Remember...!" I heard the echoes in my head. *But how could this be?* I questioned further. *Isn't everybody in America supposed to be rich and live in luxury? And shouldn't "everybody" include my father as well?* That's what everybody back home told me. And everyone who knew I was emigrating to America envied my good fortune, and wished they could change places with me. Now fully awake, the truth about my American father's financial situation was becoming clearer by each passing minute....

From what I've seen so far, my father was neither rich nor well off, and he certainly did not live in luxury. Judging from his blistered hands I noticed when I first met him, he worked very hard for every-thing he had and appreciated simple things in life other people might take for granted—the indoor bathroom with a bathtub and hot water, his three-room tiny apartment he had shared with a roommate until now. And, of course, his pride and joy featherbed he let me have to sleep on—until the bed and bureau he ordered for me arrives. My father was not rich. But he was proud and honorable, I concluded.

Now that one of his three children was with him, it was plain to see he was as proud as the proudest peacock in the barnyard and as happy as the day he married his childhood sweetheart—my mother. Being clear about these facts, I decided to keep to myself any negative feelings about my new home. Anyway, the fact that my father was not rich nor well-off didn't bother me, but it did surprise me. Especially when I recalled "me" as a child, running around barefoot and in tattered clothes just as all other children I played with did, and no one else was teased about it but I had to endure the painful ribbing about my "rich father in America who lived in luxury."

I grew up under meager circumstances—no better or worse from everybody else in the village. But I never felt deprived, because I knew of no other way of life. In addition, the abundance of natural beauty around me more than made up for what I might have lacked. I thrived on limited but good food, unpolluted mountain air, spring water from pristine woodlands, and the joy I experienced running through the meadows decorated by a profusion of wildflowers every spring, summer, and autumn. I couldn't even imagine life, without grass, flowers and trees. "Please God, let there be a garden, grass, and trees on the ground below our apartment, and let it be an extension of my humble new home," I prayed until it was time to get up.

As soon as the early morning sun illuminated my empty, tiny room and birds began to chirp, I left the featherbed and ran to the small corner window in my room. I was anxious to see what was on the ground below. I was hoping, with all my heart, I would find at least a small garden where spring flowers bloomed. Or maybe an apple and a cherry tree boasting white and pink blossoms. But when I stuck my head out the window, the only thing I saw was the unattractive black roof of another building. The garden, grass, and trees must be below the window in my father's room, I dared to dream.

I tiptoed to the kitchen so I wouldn't disturb my father, still sleeping behind the closed door in his room, and checked again the view from the kitchen window facing the roof. I opened the curtain, quickly closed it shut, and vowed always to keep it closed. Nothing had changed since the day before. I had not overlooked anything important on the roof facing the kitchen window, except a few wooden boxes filled to the rim with dirt and several scrawny-looking barely visible plants—no good reason for keeping the curtain open. And I didn't bother opening the curtain on the other kitchen window facing the street.

Soon my father awakened and greeted me with a big smile. "Good morning, Luba! Did you sleep well on my fluffy featherbed?" he wanted to know.

I smiled back and told him, "The featherbed was very comfortable." I was glad he didn't ask again how I liked my new home. I then helped him prepare our first breakfast together—oatmeal mixed with milk, two soft boiled eggs, toast, and tea. While we ate, we discussed my trip to America and I brought him up-to-date on the family back home. After a leisurely breakfast, my father called me over to the window in his room and opened it. I was sure he wanted to show me the backyard enhanced by a garden, and a grassy patch where blooming trees waved in spring breezes.

"Luba, any clothes you need to dry after you wash them in the bathtub—you'll find the scrubbing board there too—this is where you'll hang them," he instructed. There, on a wheel attached to the side of the window in his room, was a long line that extended to another wheel attached to a tall wooden pole resting against the wall of a weathered brownstone building across the yard—littered with tin cans, bottles, rags, and paper, suffocating the sparse blades of wild grasses peeking from under the trash. There was no garden, blossoming trees, or spring flowers below my father's bedroom window, either. My spirit plummeted further. Especially when my father told me the backyard belonged to the people who owned the tavern facing the lot, so I couldn't even attempt a cleanup. And even if the lot didn't belong to anyone in particular, "there is no access to it from our apartment," he informed me sadly. He must have seen the disappointment on my face, even though I tried hard not to show it. Now that I had seen everything there was to see and found nothing to uplift my downtrodden spirit, I questioned my new life with my father.

Tears filled my eyes. To hold them back from spilling over, I changed the subject to happier times we both might still remember. We reminisced about the splendors of the changing seasons back home in our Carpathian Mountains. And when I saw my father drying his eyes, I finally let go of my suppressed tears. We both cried, but for different reasons. I made sure mine was not revealed to him at the time. The morning passed quickly. It was time for my first lunch with my father in America and I wondered what kind of food he would serve—hopefully not anything from the ocean, still alive.

A knock on the door interrupted our lunch of ham and cheese on a roll and a cup of tea. "I have a present for Luba," said the man who moved his things out of my room the evening before. He then hand-ed me a tall interesting-looking mint-green tin can decorated with pictures of fancy ladies holding umbrellas and scattered dark-brown double disks with white filling between them. Even though the tin can felt too light to have anything in it, I anxiously pulled off the cover expecting to find something inside. To my surprise, disappointment, and even embarrassment, there was nothing to be had. But a present is still a present, I reasoned, so I thanked my father's former room-mate just the same. And I assured him I would put the tin can to good use—whatever that might be.

"This is not a very nice gift," my father complained after his for-mer roommate left our apartment, and while examining the tin can to make sure he didn't overlook anything inside it, he appeared upset. "Such a thoughtless individual! He ate the Oreo cookies inside the tin can, and gave you an empty tin for a present. How insensitive!"

"Speaking of presents, I have to tell you something," I said to my father as I opened my carry-all bag and took out the orange. "This is all I have for you," I confessed as I handed him the orange. "I was bringing you several strings of dried mushrooms from our own forest back home—some I picked myself—but the mushrooms were confis-cated by the Customs. I'm sorry!" I told him. My father's eyes flood-ed with tears again. He seemed more touched by the gift he did not receive than by the one he received—the big, beautiful orange! He said "Thanks for the orange," and placed it on top of the other fruit in a bowl set atop a small counter next to the kitchen sink. He then took off his glasses, dried his moist eyes and announced:

"Luba, get ready, we're going shopping. You deserve a gift too, something you'll remember and enjoy for a very long time." And my father and I went shopping together for the first time—my second day in America. It was an excursion of a life time! I walked close to him while my eyes feasted on things all around me—everything so new and so exciting: brownstone buildings with large windows enhanced by pretty white lace curtains; tiny gardens around the steps of some buildings with spring flowers ready to bloom or in bloom and some boasting budding rosebushes…. But I didn't see any cascading flowers from those so-called fire escapes, which I thought were balconies. And I did not see money growing on trees or sidewalks lined with gold as some people back home erroneously believed.

Once we reached what I considered a marketplace, I didn't know which way to look. There was so much to see and marvel at. Display windows boasting beautiful things to wear, eat, amuse with…. And when my father purchased a fabulous record player for me and several great Ukrainian and Polish records (the languages I was proficient in besides my Lemko-Rusyn) and paid cash for everything, I decided he couldn't be as poor as my first impressions suggested. Back home my family could never afford to buy such items of luxury and pay outright for them, no matter how hard they worked. Maybe this is the reason America is known throughout the world as the land of opportunity, it occurred to me. You have an opportunity to earn enough money to treat yourself to luxury items and to a good life. Finally, something was beginning to make some sense!

"Your present is meant to serve a dual purpose, Luba—a welcome-to-America gift and a Happy Sixteenth Birthday! In America sixteenth birthdays are considered milestones in young peoples' lives. Traditionally speaking, you reached your first milestone on May 10th, Luba," he pointed out, as we carried home my treasured gifts. Back home we didn't celebrate birthdays—no reason to celebrate getting older, people reasoned. Therefore I didn't feel neglected or left out when this, according to my father, "milestone" birthday came and went—coincidentally, around the time I was leaving for America—and nothing special was done for me. But my Americanized father saw things from a different perspective. Lucky for me!

My record player became my saving grace once my father went back to work after a few days at home following my arrival. It was to that wonderful gift I turned to for company on lonely days and evenings I had to spend by myself. And there were many such days and evenings, since my father worked nights and slept in the daytime. I saw him mostly on weekends only. On Sunday afternoons we usually visited my father's friends, one of them being Harry and his wife, the man who picked me up from the airport when I arrived in America. On the first visit to their home, the couple presented me with a beautiful sculptured Holy Family statue—one of my treasured possessions to this day. We would also visit my mother's sister, Aunt Mary, and her married children. Aunt Mary always welcomed us with a cheerful smile and offered us something good to eat she herself prepared. On occasions the same people paid us visits back. But regardless of who visited who, my father almost always put me on display—not a good thing to do to a sixteen-year-old young lady.

"Look at my daughter, isn't she beautiful! Take a look at her gorgeous locks of blonde hair—note those lovely ringlets," he would boast. During those times, I wished the floor beneath me would open up and make me disappear. If that wasn't enough embarrassment, he would also ask me to sing for people on occasions. "Doesn't my Luba sing like a bird in spring?" he would ask my audience and expect a positive reply. Often I felt sorry for him because he acted as if he was the only man in the world who had sired a child and was now a "Daddy." It seemed he could hardly believe it himself, so he flaunted that fact on anybody who would listen, just to hear himself say, "I am a father, and I have been all along, and here's the proof. God willing, additional proof will come at a later date."

After a few displays of my father's overzealous pride, I eventually mustered enough courage to tell him his excessive pride was humiliating me. But even my forthrightness didn't completely take care of what was becoming a big problem for me. A shy sixteen-year-old girl uprooted at a very critical time in her life, trying to fit into a society not of her background. Finally, I decided to take the reins into my own hands and handle each new situation my way.

If my father praised my blonde curly hair, I told the truth: "my hair was permed and it will soon be straight." If he asked me to sing for people, I gracefully declined, saying: "I am sure these wonderful folks have better things to do—or talk about—than to listen to me sing." It worked! I was able to solve the problem without really hurting my father's delicate feelings. But I couldn't solve my other problems—the ones of loneliness and despair.

As May turned to June and then to July, my loneliness, along with the hot weather, became unbearable. Most nights I cried myself to sleep. Time stood still for me. One day was an exact copy of the day before. Each sunrise was a beginning of a lonely day and each sunset an end to a lonely day. The passing time didn't seem to lessen my longing for the family and friends I left behind, as I hoped it would— it only intensified it. Physically, I lived with my father in a third floor apartment in Jersey City. Mentally, I kept on returning to my family and friends, with whom half of my spirit chose to remain, and to my beloved mountains, from which the other half refused to depart.

Back in my mountain home in thought, I tended the cattle in the pasture by the forest, rejoiced in the fields of blooming potato plants, giggled at the rows of toppling cabbage heads, and danced in rhythm with gently swaying waves of wheat, barley, and oats. And in another part of the world, where my family lived now, Peter reached for my hand while we watched the red sun slowly slipping behind the mountains of rubble and cement waiting to be raised up again to the city's pre-war glory, as he and I dreamed of the glory of our own, someday. Too soon the reality would step in and nudge me to return to the present. And I'd be back in the apartment my father and I shared, whether I wanted to or not, because this was my home now.

To contend with my loneliness, I began reading books written in Slavic languages I understood. I found them in a special section of the local public library. When I wasn't making meals, washing and ironing clothes, or listening to my favorite records, I read my books. Through them l always managed to temporarily escape from my lonely existence. And when the pesky mosquitoes discovered the screenless window in my room and wouldn't let me sleep at night, I turned to my precious autograph book. I read it from cover to cover many times over, spending extra time on the page where Peter drew me a picture. The picture of a country cottage with a white picket fence and sunflowers smiling under the bright sun helped me dream happy dreams when I finally fell asleep—dreams that would forever remain just "dreams." On those sleepless nights I also entertained thoughts of going back home. *What am I doing here, anyway?* Life was passing me by—the precious years of my youth I could never reclaim—yet I felt powerless to do anything about it at the time.

Every day I checked the mailbox on the ground-floor by the entrance door, and every day I found it empty. *Why isn't anybody writing to me? Don't my mother and brothers miss me as much as I miss them and want to know how I'm doing?* I had already written several letters to them, but received replies to none.

One day at the mailbox I met an elderly neighbor lady and her daughter who lived above us on the top floor (fourth). Prior to this day I saw them only in passing; otherwise I avoided them because almost every day I heard an uproar coming from their apartment which used to scare me half to death at times.

Finding an empty mailbox yet another day reduced me to tears while the two neighbor ladies watched. I guess they felt sorry for me and as a result invited me up to their place. Both women spoke some Czechoslovakian so we understood each other. Any other time I would have gracefully declined their invitation, because they were not the kind of people I wanted to make friends with. On this day, however, I felt exceptionally lonely and vulnerable and I agreed to visit with the two women.

As soon as I entered their apartment—an exact copy of ours—the younger woman (daughter) began to complain about her former husband. Before long, she brought out the wedding picture of the two of them, and with a butcher knife cut out her ex-husband from the picture, leaving herself intact. She then placed the photo of him, alone, on the kitchen table and began throwing daggers at it. Finally, with the same butcher knife she finished the job, reducing his likeness to shreds.

I feared for my life! I thought about running out, but the fire in the younger woman's eyes made me rethink that option. I breathed a sigh of relief when, after ten minutes or so (an eternity to me) the two women—mother and daughter—began fighting between themselves and seemed to have forgotten I was even there. I slipped out without their noticing I had left. I tiptoed downstairs, bolted the door to our apartment, and vowed to keep it bolted at all times. Safely at home, I fell to my knees and thanked my guardian angel for watching over me when I was in danger. And I learned a valuable lesson that day I vowed never to forget—don't let your emotions make you do something you know is wrong!

Days passed but nothing in my life was changing. June 1949 turned to July and I knew as much English as the day I arrived in America. None! I was not only lonely, I was also depressed. Once again, I allowed my emotional state to make me do something I knew deep down was wrong and vowed never to repeat, because I had already learned my lesson. I accepted an invitation from a very old woman who lived on the floor below us to visit with her in her apartment and "spend some quality time together," as she put it. She seemed to understand my Lemko-Rusyn language when I spoke to her by the mailbox on several occasions in the past. And except for her odd dress habits, enhanced by enormous amounts of shiny jewelry, she appeared to have all her faculties intact. Sadly, as soon as I entered her apartment I knew I had made another mistake.

Her entire kitchen was cluttered with newspapers—pile upon pile from floor to ceiling, with only a narrow pathway leading to the bathroom and to each of her two bedrooms. And God only knew what was in those bedrooms! I realized I was just as wrong about my downstairs neighbor as I was about the mother and daughter team on the top floor when the old woman reached into her apron pocket—a part of her daily dress—and pulled out a book of matches. She handed me the matches and asked me to start a fire so she could get rid of the clutter in her apartment—her newspapers and who knows what else that was lurking from beneath. Frightened, I took the matches and slowly shuffled backwards to the door leading to the hallway and just as slowly and carefully opened it. Then, like a scared rabbit, I ran upstairs to my safe haven apartment and bolted the door behind me. Once again I had a good reason to get down to my knees and thank my invisible friend—my guardian angel—watching over me. The one I would trust to get me safely back home to my mother and brothers—the sooner the better, please God, I prayed.

Following my last unpleasant experience with neighbors, I was left with a dilemma. How to tell my father the truth about my encounters with the neighbors on the top floor and the one living below us, and still retain his trust. I wrestled with many different options for several days, and then I heard the news:

The aged woman had peacefully passed away in her sleep. As for the mother/daughter duo, I never did find out what really happened to them. By coincidence, when the neighbor-lady downstairs passed, the mother/daughter team took off, too. Much like the confused aged woman downstairs, they also departed for an unknown location. Hopefully, both emotionally disturbed neighbors found the peace they lacked living where they lived—above and below our apartment. One thing for sure, their demise left room for me to plant my own seeds of peace, which would eventually grow and bloom like the unexpected garden of radiant flowers I would soon discover on another neighbor's rooftop, across from my kitchen window.

One sunny day in July 1949 I decided to give our drab-looking apartment a fresh look—maybe the nicer-looking place would make me feel less lonely and depressed, I thought. I opened the box which contained a lamp boasting a flowered shade that my father received as a reward for doing most of his grocery-shopping in a certain store. I placed the lamp in the middle of the kitchen table and on the wall above the pretty lamp I hung a scenic picture I found in the clothes closet in my room. The next step in beautifying our home was to remove, wash, and iron all the curtains. I decided to remove the curtains from the kitchen window facing the roof first. Lo and behold, I literally had to pinch myself to make sure I was not dreaming, seeing what I saw on the rooftop directly across from me.

Smiling at me—practically within my reach—were boxes of cascading red, pink, purple, and white petunias, covering almost the entire rooftop. A field of beauty I thought could only be found in the meadows of our Carpathian Mountains in spring. And I swore I heard them whisper to me. "Luba, we're here for you—the garden you've been looking for. You don't have to feel lonely and depressed any longer. If we can grow on a tarred rooftop in shallow soil and still smile and experience joy, so can you go on living where you live." As I stared at my newly discovered garden, I felt my mood lifting and my spirit soaring, as I cried tears of joy for the first time in America. I found my Blossoms on a Rooftop which inspired me to begin turning my lonely life around—one day and one step at a time.

Chapter 8

Reaching Out

It's uncanny; the moment I discovered the petunia garden on the rooftop my life changed for the better. I found myself singing again while doing the mundane chores around the house—cooking, cleaning, washing clothes, ironing…. Even my aloneness no longer had the power to drive me to despair. The sight of the flower garden on the rooftop blessed me with a brand new view of the world beyond my kitchen window. Also, strange as it may seem, from a distance the lady who tenderly cared for her petunia garden looked very much like my own mother, and even though I never met her nor did I ever know her name, on some spiritual level I visited with her on daily basis. The labor of love this enigmatic human being put into her garden of shimmering petunias year in and year out profoundly and positively affected my life. Through her love of flowers, she created and ultimately left a legacy, which in my case became my saving grace on this side of the ocean. It is, therefore, my fervent prayer that the legacy I may leave behind will touch other lives in equal measures—whatever that might be.

As the summer days marched on and the petunias continued to grace my world with their vibrant blooms, I realized they grew and bloomed because it was their time to do so. Nature had designated a specific season for them just for that purpose. Once their time for growing and blooming was over, they would grow and bloom no more. One hot summer afternoon as I contemplated these truths, it occurred to me that perhaps there was a season for me to do the same—grow and bloom—and that season was the present time for me to begin learning English and other things in my new surroundings. The seed for learning English and for transition into an American way of life was finally planted—thanks to the petunia garden on the rooftop. I felt confident each would take root because I was ready to begin!

One Saturday morning, the latter part of August 1949, my father went food-shopping, his usual chore on his day off from work since I was unable to do so during the week due to a language barrier. He sent me shopping once with a list of items, only to have me return empty-handed with tears in my eyes. Instead of a grocery store, I stopped in a candy store to buy milk, bread, eggs, and cold cuts. Needless to say, the humiliation became too much for me to try another food-shopping expedition. I preferred instead to stay at home and cook while my father shopped.

This particular day I chose to make one of my father's favorite foods—*perohy* (ravioli-like dumplings). When he returned with bags full of groceries, I had the *perohy* lined up on the kitchen table in perfect rows, like soldiers ready for inspection. In the past my father could hardly wait until I served him this special dish, but this day he offered to cook the *perohy* himself and seemed anxious to tell me something:

"Luba, I happened to run to an old friend of mine in the store," my father said while unpacking the groceries. "Her daughter Nina goes to the school you'll be going to and she speaks our Lemko-Rusyn language, too. Nina and her mother are going shopping for school clothes and supplies for Nina, later on today—school is only a couple of weeks away, you know. She invited you to come along." He studied my expression and added, "They'll be passing our house and will ring our bell. Be ready to leave when you hear the bell, if you'd like to go with them. Otherwise, they'll leave without you," he warned. My face must have lit up when I heard I might be going shopping with people who spoke my language, because my father opened his wallet and handed me a dollar bill to buy something for myself, too. But he cautioned not to waste the dollar on anything useless or frivolous. "Save the dollar for a rainy day, if you don't see anything you really want and need," he urged.

"But I already saved enough money for that day," I protested. "In my Oreo cookie tin (the empty tin can I received as a present upon my arrival in America) are lots of nickels, dimes and even a few quarters I earned for ironing your shirts—that's all rainy-day money. Do I have to save this dollar too? Anyway, I don't even know what one dollar can buy," I argued.

"Have a nice time shopping and don't buy junk," my father said with a smile.

I twisted the paper dollar bill in my hands for several seconds before placing it in my pocket. I was hoping he would break down and double or even triple my shopping money, but the tactics didn't work. The memory of the Great Depression of the late 1920's and early 1930's left a lasting fear of the bread and soup lines in my father's mind. He remained overly frugal for the rest of his life and denied himself all things that, in his estimation, cost too much money or he could do without. The money he saved when he finally got a job after the Depression became a security blanket he traveled with throughout the rest of his life. The doorbell rang and I hurried downstairs to meet my father's friend and her daughter.

"I'm Rose and this is my daughter Nina. You must be Luba—your father told me all about you. We're happy to meet you," said Nina's mother with a smile while Nina kept on fidgeting.

"Yes! I'm Luba and I'm pleased to meet you both, too," I said, extending my hand to greet them. To my surprise, Nina's mother embraced me and lovingly hugged me as if she'd just found her long-lost daughter. Nina awkwardly shook my hand and nudged her mother to get going. She seemed eager to hit the stores.

Nina's mom seemed very sweet and I took an instant liking to her. A short, stocky, bubbly, middle-age lady with graying brown, tightly-permed hair and wide-rimmed glasses; she talked incessantly. Nina, on the other hand, had very little to say, except to dictate to her mother what she wanted to buy for school in terms of clothes. I thought she was somewhat spoiled, and seemed immature for her age—almost fourteen, her mother told me. "I became sixteen on May 10th," I told them.

Nina's mother bought everything Nina tried on and liked. When she finally finished shopping she had: Long circular felt skirts; pleated skirts; blouses and sweaters to match the skirts; ballerina shoes and black-seamed stockings; regular flat shoes and white socks…. Everything looked beautiful on Nina's slender, tall body.

Nina's mother didn't seem to mind spending lots of money on her daughter—unlike my father who hesitated to part with his. Maybe her husband and she didn't live through the Great Depression like he did, I reasoned. She even bought me a summer print blouse that I liked but it would have taken my whole dollar to buy. "A present from me and Nina for you, so you can spend your money on something else you might find and like," she said. To this day—over half a century later—I still remember that sleeveless summer blouse, with delicate pink flowers and green leaves which reminded me of the wildflowers that grew in the meadows back home. But most of all I remember the kind lady who gave me that unexpected gift—Nina's mother, Rose.

On the way home, we stopped in a place called the Five and Ten Cent Store to buy notebooks, pencils, and erasers for school for Nina. "This will complete my shopping list for school," I heard her say to her mother after she purchased everything on her list.

While Nina and her mother shopped for school supplies for Nina, I went browsing around the store to see what I could buy for my dollar. That's when I stumbled upon the section of children's books—that magical part of childhood I had missed when I was growing up. I opened several beautifully illustrated hard-cover Golden Books and became fascinated by the make-believe world of childhood I had not been fortunate enough to experience. Could I still relive moments of that special period of my life and learn to read, write, and understand a few simple English words at the same time? I wondered! I was sure my father would be happy to help me get started. And I envisioned the two of us working together, making up for the time we were absent from each other's lives. What a great idea! I thought.

I checked the prices on the Golden Books. How fortunate I had enough money to buy at least four books, I thought, and still have a few pennies left over. I chose the books with the most meaningful and colorful illustrations. I was proud of myself and was sure my father would be proud of me, too, because I didn't waste my money on useless or frivolous things. Nina looked at my books with a peculiar smirk

71

and then told me what she thought of my purchases: "I read novels not baby books like some people I know," she boasted and giggled, looking over my shoulder. Her mother heard her.

"You will apologize to Luba for your rudeness," Nina's mother demanded. Nina's freckled face turned red and she gave her mother and me a look that could kill. Her mother returned the killer look and waited until Nina mumbled under her breath, "I'm sorry, Luba." But then she jerked her brown-haired head and sputtered fire from her large, beautiful brown eyes at her mother and at me. Nina's mother became angry again. She stepped in front of Nina and in a raised voice spoke.

"Nina, your behavior is obnoxious and I would like to see it stopped right now! Be sure when we get home we will have a long discussion about this day. I would like to hear a real apology to Luba this time so the two of you could be friends," she said sternly. "Heaven knows you can use a nice friend," she sighed.

Nina assumed a far-away look and muttered something that sounded like an apology, but I questioned it. And I wondered what she was thinking and feeling. Was she jealous because her mother seemed to like me as much as I liked her? Should I step aside for Nina's sake and my peace? Or should I try to develop friendship with Nina, as her mother suggested? But the truth was we were so different from each other and I wondered if friendship between us was even possible.

I wanted a friend like Pauline whose friendship I treasured still, even though we were worlds apart and most likely would never see or hear from each other again. But Nina was not Pauline and my expectations of her were unrealistic, I admitted to myself. I could try to be Nina's friend, if she would be willing to open up her world to me and accept me for myself. We could then begin learning from each other and about each other; find a common ground where seeds of friendship could be planted, nurtured so they could grow and bloom like the petunias on the rooftop. I would give it a try. Heaven knows I needed a friend, too. I reasoned silently.

I was happy to find my father at home when I returned from that memorable shopping trip with Nina and her mother. I could hardly wait to show him what I had bought for my dollar—how wisely I spent my money. Excited, I emptied my shopping bag on the table in front of my father, who was engrossed in his Lemko newspaper—*The Karpatska Rus*—at the time.

"Look what I bought for the money you gave me!" I pointed to my books, excitedly. "These beautiful children's books will make learning English easy and fun. Don't you agree?" I felt genuinely happy and I wanted to share that happiness with my father but it appeared he wanted no part of it, which puzzled me. He looked at my purchases with only one eye; the other eye remained covered by his newspaper. I tried again to get his attention and reaction to my treasures.

"I can hardly wait to start learning English, but I'll need some help from you. How would you like to be my first English teacher?" I asked with a smile, and expected a smile in return. My father finally let go of his newspaper, wrinkled up his face, and began scrutinizing my valuables—the children's books I bought and the flowered blouse Nina's mother bought for me. Without saying a word, he shoved the books to the side, furrowed his forehead and focused his attention on the blouse—the one item I didn't buy.

"What's wrong? You seem upset, but why?" I questioned him. He held up the blouse and sputtered what was bothering him.

"You'll get some use out of the blouse but you wasted the rest of the money," he said angrily, scattering my books all over the table before he went on. "Something I didn't want you to do—waste money. These books are for young children, not for someone your age," he said gruffly. "Make sure they're returned and the money is put away for a rainy day," he ordered and buried his face in his newspaper again. Then without uttering another word, he picked himself up and disappeared behind the closed door of his room. I was stunned by the way my father reacted to my precious books and I saw my short-lived happy world fall apart again.

Overtaken by mental anguish, I sat in front of the kitchen window overlooking the petunia garden. Gazing in the direction of the blossoms, I wondered what I should do. Follow my father's orders and return the books, or follow my own instincts and keep the books. The petunia blossoms I focused on seemed unaffected by my sullen mood. Their rainbow-color faces were even more radiant than when I admired them last. And yet, they reached that state of perfection without anyone dictating to them what tools to use to get there. My mind was made up!

I was ready to tell my father—with all due respect—"I'm keeping the books! You gave me the money to buy what I needed and liked, and that's what I did. You can't expect me to run back to the store to return them now. I'm not going to do that, because that's not fair." I would tell my father exactly how I felt; I was angry too! I was about to knock on his bedroom door when he opened it.

"Luba, I have a confession to make, please sit down." He pointed to the chair by the kitchen table. I didn't know what to expect or what spurred this confession. But I did as he asked. He sat on the only other chair in our kitchen. With bowed head and obvious uneasiness, he began:

"As you know, I've been in America for a very long time, since the early 1920's, with the exception of several trips back home long enough for each of you to be born. You probably assume, and with good reason, that I am completely fluent in the English language and able to write and read, too. I must tell you," my father said in a quivering voice, "I speak only broken English and can't read or write. I became upset when I saw you bring home those books because I sensed you were going to ask me for help, and, of course, you should have, but unfortunately I can't help you. I am so ashamed to have to tell you this and I am sorry for reacting as I did." His hands shaking, he collected the books strewn all over the table and stacked them neatly. "You chose beautifully illustrated children's books and I am sure the words depicting each picture are just as beautiful. Once you learn how to read them, maybe you can teach me," my father joshed.

My father's confession touched me deeply. It was true I assumed he was fluent in the language of the country which accepted him as one of its own (he was very proud of his American Citizenship). And it was true I assumed he was able to read and write in the language of his adopted country. I also assumed he was rich, but that was not so, either. But it didn't matter that all my assumptions were wrong; he was still my father and he loved me, and that was no assumption. But since he was in the confessional mood, I did want to know as much about his life as he was willing to share with me. And so when he continued to talk, I listened:

"I came to America penniless. To survive and have a roof over my head, I took odd jobs—mostly I washed dishes in restaurants I could walk to. I saved every leftover penny to send home to help your mother take care of the farm and our young family." My father took off his glasses, dried his teary eyes and went on.

"Life was tough back home in the mountains at the time but even tougher in America. Without knowing the language, I could only find menial jobs that paid menial wages. And there was no time to go to school to learn to speak correctly, read, or write because I had to work double shifts to make ends meet. I crossed the ocean several times and even bought additional land and forest back home for the money I was able to save working in America. I did that because I didn't know where we would finally settle. Your mother loved the mountains (I did too) and being near her own mother and sisters made her happy, so I never insisted that she leave her family, pack up the children and go to America with me."

"During the Great Depression," my father continued, "I stood on bread and soup lines with everybody else because I couldn't make enough money to make a living. Finally, I temporarily moved to Upstate New York to work for room and board on my sister's farm. She had small children at the time and I picked up enough English from them to help me move up the ladder in the labor force when the Great Depression finally ended."

"After making another trip overseas—that's when you were born—" he poured himself a glass of water, took a sip of it and went on—"I returned to America and got a job in construction, my kind of work and money too. My last trip back home was when you were about five or six years old and it was also my shortest. After only several weeks at home, I barely escaped from Hitler's clutches." My father sighed and went on, "During the war I worked in shipyards. I was the one who built scaffolding for the ship-builders. I fell off of one of those scaffolds and it was only by the Grace of God that I survived. Every bone in my body seemed to be broken and I was placed in a body cast and left to live or die in the hospital for many months.

I was in and out of comas at first and when I was strong enough to fight to live, I fought with all my might because I wanted to see my family again. It paid off, but I could never again do the work I loved— ship-building." My father took another sip of water and continued.

"I then ventured into a partnership in the saloon business. I realized that the saloon business was not for me and after only a year or so I pulled out. I learned weaving and got a job operating huge machines making beautiful velvet." My father's face lit up as he talked about his latest, and what seemed a very satisfying job. He then excused himself and a few minutes later came back with pieces of exquisite velvet. "Samples of my work," he boasted.

The summary of his life came to an end, but I wished there was more, because it allowed me to travel with him through the years and helped me to understand why he lived his life the way he did and learned only what he learned—broken English and no reading or writing. But he was proud of his accomplishments in other areas and so was I.

When I saw my father was done reminiscing, I decided to bring up the subject of school. I asked him if he knew of someone who could help me learn some basic English before the start of school, which was only days away. "We could begin with my children's books," I suggested.

"I do know a retired teacher who speaks a little Polish and who may be able to help you. Her name is Alice and she lives in an apartment with her elderly parents a few blocks from us. I'll check with her right now to see if she'd give you some English lessons before school starts," he said, while getting ready to pay Alice a visit and motioning me to come along.

Alice agreed to give me a one-hour lesson each day of the week until school opened—about nine or ten lessons in all. I offered to help pay for the lessons, but my father wouldn't hear of it. "The money in your Oreo cookie tin is for a rainy day—this is not one of them," he insisted. But we didn't have to worry about paying for the lessons; Alice offered to give me the lessons free of charge, "my contribution to Luba's education," she told us. On the way home my father said he would buy Alice a nice present at the end of my lessons. I felt happy and proud of him.

My first lesson with Alice was learning the alphabet which I mastered quickly because it was similar to the one I already knew. The next few lessons were learning to read, write, and understand what was written in my children's books, which I brought with me to each lesson. The last couple of lessons were spent on learning the numbers one to ten, days of the week, seasons and months of the year, and greetings such as good morning, good evening and good night. When I completed all the lessons, I had in my vocabulary about one hundred or so English words. And I worked very hard to accomplish that much. Would this be enough to begin school with? Time would tell.

My father gave Alice a huge box of chocolates and a gold cross as a token of our appreciation. And I wrote a short thank-you note in my limited English to accompany the presents. Alice surprised me with a present of her own, a dual-type dictionary: Polish-English and English-Polish, the language I was most proficient in besides Ukrainian and Lemko-Rusyn I spoke at home.

This extraordinary gift from Alice—the dictionary—represented to me an extension of Alice herself, since it was there for me each time I needed to look up a meaning of a word. I have not forgotten Alice and never will. She helped me start the foundation upon which my future education in America would rest—much like the lady in the apartment across from my kitchen window and her petunia garden on the rooftop which inspired me to go forward and to grow. Thank you, Alice—wherever you are—for your good deeds on my behalf. Through the years I did my best to follow your good example and I promise to continue.

Chapter 9

Beginning of School

My father re-soled and replaced the worn-out heels on my black suede shoes in preparation for the new experience I was about to undertake—the beginning of school. The day before, I washed and ironed the print cotton dress I had worn when I arrived in America, and happily proclaimed to the world around me—an empty room in this case—"I am all ready to start school in the morning!" And then, out of the blue, visions of Nina's specially chosen school clothes—latest style skirts, sweaters, blouses, shoes—on Nina's tall slender body, preoccupied my mind.

I held the floral cotton dress next to the old black suede shoes and I panicked. If Nina was an example of what the other girls would wear on the first day of school and thereafter, I was in big trouble. An outdated cotton dress on my back and shoes that have seen better days on my feet—coupled with my extremely limited English—would surely place me in a class all by myself and for all the wrong reasons. The grim picture I painted for myself refused to budge from my thoughts, even though I desperately tried to change the scene by closing my eyes and imagining myself in a stylish new dress and shoes, looking as great as Nina and other girls might look in my new school. But deep down I knew I was fooling myself. And for me this situation would not change any time soon, because my father made it clear:

"The shoes and the dress have a lot of wear left in them and are good enough for the first day of school and at least for one more year. We can't be wasteful, you know," he reaffirmed. But I silently disagreed.

The dress and the shoes would have been good enough for the first day of school, for another year and even beyond, if I were back home in the mountains. In America young people followed fashions, I had quickly discovered. But my father didn't seem to understand that. He lived by the "waste not, want not" rule and believed that as long as something fits, is kept clean and in good condition, "wear it and be grateful you have it." Was he still living in the Great Depression days? If so, was he ever going to let go of the past embrace the present and look forward to a brighter future? I questioned and worried, because his way of life affected my life, too!

If my mother were here, she would certainly see things differently; I would have a new dress and new shoes as well, just like Nina, and look as great as Nina—on the first day of school and thereafter. And only God knew what hardships she had endured—along with the rest of us—during the long war years and the post-war era, probably equal to or even greater than the Great Depression he lived through! Yet, she—as well as the rest of us—managed to leave the past behind, while he clung to his with all his might. There was no one in the room to hear and respond to my complaints and disappointments, because my father was at work. School was only hours away and I had to deal with and resolve my own doubts, uncertainties, and fears.

Once again I turned to the "Blossoms on the Rooftop" smiling at me from the neighboring rooftop, the same petunia blossoms that had inspired me to go forward when my downtrodden spirit was on the verge of giving up. Gazing at the radiant petunias, and half-listening to the clock on the wall ticking away the seconds of the late summer afternoon, bringing me closer to that formidable first day of school, my eyes fell on blossoms I had not noticed before. Sprinkled in between the solid color blossoms of red, pink, purple, and white were multicolor blooms whose variegated faces added an extra special touch to an already beautiful garden, transforming it to an extraordinary one.

Ironically, the colors of the multicolor blossoms—which further enhanced the garden—matched the colors of the flowers in my dress, which made me rethink my worrisome as well as fearful situation. If the multicolor petunias—different from the rest of their siblings and cousins—made such a positive difference in the petunia world, maybe my flower-dress and newly repaired old shoes would also blend in with different colors and styles in the people's world, those worn by the girls in my new school, including Nina. That is, if I held my head high, proud of who I was—Luba, who left her homeland to come to America to live with her father, who spoke very little English, wearing her native dress. Was there anything wrong with that picture? My answer was a definite No! I took another look at my dress and shoes and saw a pretty cotton summer dress and re-soled suede shoes with new heels, "good enough for the first day of school and at least for one more year."

I uncovered from my dresser a pencil box with a few pencils and erasers in it and a notebook I bought when my father sent me to the store to buy fruit and I erroneously walked into a stationery store. Embarrassed when asked what I wanted, I pointed to pencil boxes, pencils, and notebooks. Now I was glad I had them because I had something to carry to school with me in the morning. This time I was really ready to start school.

I tried to avoid eye contact with Nina when I spotted her in line in front of the school. I was embarrassed enough that my father had to walk me to school. I didn't want Nina to make some sly comment such as: Only babies are walked to school by their fathers—especially since she knew how old I was. At least two years older than the oldest student in school, according to her. Nina saw me, anyway, and frantically waved both her hands to get my attention. At the same time, I saw her whispering something to the girl standing next to her. They both giggled and I was positive they were talking about me. I silently prayed I would not be placed in Nina's class, and worse yet, sit next to her.

My father and I walked halfway through a busy corridor before we entered an over-cluttered office with boxes. New books and school supplies protruded from the open ones. A stout, middle-aged stern-looking lady pointed to several empty chairs in the corner of the room. She instructed us to sit down and wait for the principal when my father told her he came to register me for school. The surprised look on the lady's face indicated possible problems with the registration we had not anticipated.

The principal, a pleasant-looking, also middle-aged lady, dressed in a dark blue suit and pink blouse tied into a bow at the neck, met us about a half-hour later. She introduced herself to us as Miss Robb. My father then introduced himself and me to her. He handed her the documents we brought with us and she began scrutinizing them. After several minutes, she looked up at my father and asked:

"Why didn't you register Luba for fall semester in May, when she came here?" she wanted to know.

My father shrugged his shoulders and replied, "I'm sorry, but I didn't know I needed to do it that early in the year for the upcoming semester."

"Unfortunately, we are not prepared in this school, at this late date, to handle a student who doesn't speak English," Miss Robb informed us. And after a pause she explained the reason why, pausing now and then to give my father time to translate everything to me.

"Luba needs a private tutor and we have no funds in our budget at this time to pay for one. If we knew in May she was coming to our school in September, every effort would have been made to arrange for the special help necessary for Luba to be able to survive in an all-English classroom. I regret to tell you there is nothing I can do for her now," she firmly stated, and with a hint of a smile wished us good luck.

I needed a breath of fresh air and to be alone when I realized what impact Miss Robb's decision might have on my life. My father stayed behind. "I need to talk to Miss Robb some more," he told me before I walked out. The students were in their classrooms by then so I knew there was no chance I would meet up with Nina and her friends again.

I found my sanctuary in the courtyard behind the yellow-brick school building—huge in size but with no room for me inside. I was ready to tell my father I wanted to go back home where I belonged. But when I returned to Miss Robb's office to get my father, I found him sporting a wide grin. I knew something had changed to make him smile like that, and it had.

"Miss Robb cut through a lot of red tape on your behalf, Luba," my father said in a low voice, as if he didn't want anyone else to hear. "She'll take you in on a three-month trial basis," he boasted, as if to say, "It wasn't easy, but I managed to persuade the principal to do what I know is best for my daughter."

"You will be placed in grade 8A. If you do well," my father informed me," you will graduate in January 1950 with your class and be promoted to high school," he said proudly, as if I were already there. In those days graduation was held twice a year—Class 8A graduated in January and Class 8B in June.

"If you can't grasp what is being taught," my father went on while Miss Robb looked on, "I'll have to make other arrangements for your education. But I have a feeling we won't have to worry about that," he said with a smile. He then placed a kiss on my head—something he didn't do too often. Miss Robb nodded in approval.

Miss Robb then shook my father's hand, said good-bye to him and walked me to my classroom. The teacher introduced herself to me as Miss Sallaro and then she introduced me to the class. Miss Sallaro was a slightly built lady probably my mother's age, about mid-forties. She seemed like the motherly type even though her attire was strictly professional, and because of that I thought I could like her. I missed my mom very much and looked up to any woman who reminded me of her.

"This is Luba! She speaks very little English so we need to be extra nice to her and help her in any way we can," Miss Sallaro told the class. I understood what she said and felt good about it. But that feeling was short-lived. Miss Sallaro asked for a volunteer to show me around the school and it was Nina who waved both her hands to be first in line. She got the job! My heart dropped to my toes. Not because I had anything in particular against Nina, but because I wanted a fresh start with someone who didn't know me, who would let me find my own way around. Someone who would let me make my own mistakes and learn from them, and be there for me only if I needed help. I doubted that Nina could do that. I feared she would always picture me the way I was when she first met me—helpless.

Miss Sallaro pointed to the seat in front of her desk and motioned for me to sit down; at least I wasn't sitting next to Nina. I plopped my trembling body into the seat, feeling all eyes in the classroom on me. For a brief moment I felt out of place in my flower-dress, black suede shoes, and stringy hair that needed either a fresh cut or a new perm.

But as soon as I remembered the multicolored petunias on the rooftop and the lesson I learned from them, my uneasiness subsided a little. I straightened myself up and faced the class. All the girls and boys in the classroom, filled to capacity, seemed to be dressed in up-to-date styles of the late 1940's. Girls had long skirts, matching short-sleeve sweaters or blouses, and short straight or permed hair. Boys in long pants and matching shirts sported slick short hair cuts.

I heard a few snickers from some of the classmates and was beginning to feel uneasy again. To remedy that situation and to stop the jitters that were about to make themselves visible to others and threatened to further weaken my fragile confidence, I focused on an open window to the side of me. I imagined myself as a tiny bird flying right out of that classroom without anyone noticing I was gone. I saw myself flying past my father's apartment, over the ocean and strange land, back home where everyone knew me and understood me; to another classroom far away in the mountains, or to the one I left most recently, where Peter and I exchanged glances of first love. Soon my sweet daydreams were interrupted by the sound of a bell and Nina by my side anxious to explain its meaning, And there were no more snickers from the classmates—meant to annoy me—on that first day of school, and only occasional ones from that day on. Was it because I refused to be bothered by them? Probably!

"The bell is the signal for everyone to go home for lunch," Nina said with authority. "Be back in one hour and sit in this same seat," she instructed, pointing to the seat as if I didn't know any better. She then hurried to catch up with the other girls walking home for lunch. The next day at lunch time and at the end of the school day thereafter, Nina walked home with me. She jibber-jabbered nonstop in our common Lemko language, from which she never deviated. In time I noticed that no one in class besides Nina bothered with me. It was as if I was approachable only by her. I was referred to by the other classmates as "that foreign girl who only understands Nina."

In class I caught a word here and there but not enough to know what the lesson was about, or to be able to participate in any classroom discussions. I simply just occupied the seat in the room and was left alone to listen and observe. A waste of time, I thought, because I wasn't learning anything new. I felt discriminated against, especially when I saw one of the girls in my class pointing to me and calling me a "greenhorn." Nina was there when this happened, but she did not come to my defense.

Things were not going well for me that first month of school in September of 1949. I was failing everything! I wished I could have gone back to the first day of school to start over again, but without Nina as my guide; someone who would speak to me in English. But since I couldn't go back, something had to be done about the situation I found myself in—quickly! The precious days of my three-month trial period were dwindling down and I wasn't doing what I was supposed to—learning English and mixing in with the other students.

Chapter 10

Determined to Succeed

The half-way mark of my three-month trial period in school sneaked up on me like a phantom in the night. The dead-end sign in my latest nightmare pointed directly to the classroom where I had spent the last month and a half doodling in my spiral notebook, drawing pictures of wildflowers, animals, trees,…. The message through this prophetic bad dream could not be clearer. "Stop wasting precious time in school and start learning English if you want to graduate with your classmates and be promoted to high school." Of course I wanted to be promoted to high school. I also wanted to make my father and myself proud of my accomplishments. But there were no accomplishments to speak of because I had learned practically nothing new in the first six weeks of my three-month trial period, and there were only six more weeks left before that formidable deadline. I panicked!

"Tell your father about the difficulties you're having in school, and don't waste any more time!" I heard a voice in my head say, loud and clear. "He will be disappointed at first, but will get over it. If you don't tell him now, later may be too late. Don't let that happen to you—and to your father, too!"

To soften the blow I was about to spring on my unsuspecting father and to protect my own self esteem compromised by poor performance in school thus far, I thought it would be better if I first discussed with him another bothersome concern—absence of communication between my family back home and us in America. So, on this long-ago Sunday morning at breakfast with eyes fixed on a bowl of hot oatmeal, a soft-boiled egg, toast, and tea, I blurted what up to this time I had kept to myself.

"It's been almost six months since my arrival in America and I have not received one word from Mother, Michael, and John. I am sick with worries and I miss them terribly. Do you suppose something is really wrong?" I inquired of my father, holding back the tears. He thought a minute before he replied.

"If something bad had happened back home you can be sure we would have been notified via a telegram. The truth is, it's too soon after the war for any kind of normalcy in the world, especially within the postal system," my father explained and expected me to understand. Judging by the puzzled look on my face, he probably realized his explanation was not sufficient to put my mind at ease, so he went on.

"During the war, civilian communication between countries was nonexistent. I had no way of knowing how you all fared during those difficult years or if you had survived the atrocities of the war we heard about here in the United States. I had not heard from you in seven years, and you, Luba, complain about a few months!" he emphasized and went on since my silence must have indicated I needed to hear more.

"You must be patient and not worry so much. A letter will come when you stop waiting for it. One fine day when you least expect it, you will open the mail box and find it there waiting for us both—trust me. Imagine how surprised you will be." In my estimation, my father made light of what to me was no light matter, which only added to my frustration.

"Six months without a word from Mother, Michael and John is an eternity!" I argued. But no matter how I tried to make my father understand what I was feeling, I was not convinced he did, so I left it at that. Anyway, it was time to approach another subject of grave concern—my problems in school. Gulping down the last tablespoon of oatmeal, I sputtered words I never thought I would have to hear myself say to my father.

"I'm having problems in school. I don't understand what's going on in class. No one except Nina talks to me or bothers with me and she refuses to speak to me in English. While Nina is getting more proficient in our Lemko language, I'm not learning anything new in

86

English," I told my father, and waited for his reaction. His behavior shocked me! Without saying a word, he turned away from me and assumed a deep and serious look, which frightened me. As if that was not enough, he began scratching his head and pacing the floor, rhythmically back and forth like a pendulum on a grandfather's clock. His stooped frame looked as if suddenly the problems of the whole world had fallen upon his shoulders and he was being crushed by their tremendous weight.

It's all my fault! My father put his trust in me and I failed him miserably, I blamed myself. He is so disappointed in my poor performance in school, he can't even speak or look at me. I should have kept the secret of my problems in school to myself. I chastised myself. And the longer he paced the kitchen floor, the longer my list of unpleasant thoughts grew until my mind became overtaken by unparalleled guilt. And it wasn't until he stopped pacing the floor and scratching his head, faced me and spoke to me again—after what seemed like forever—that the guilt I created in my mind began to subside.

"Luba, I would like you to take a walk with me and visit a few friends on the way," he said with a desperate look in his eyes. I liked the idea of the walk but I wasn't happy about visiting the people. I didn't want to waste my precious time making idle conversations with folks I hardly knew and some I didn't know, on a beautiful autumn afternoon when I had more important issues to talk over with my father—my problems in school. But I was relieved and grateful he was speaking to me again, and I wanted him to know that, so I agreed to go along even if it meant sitting in people's houses, listening to boring conversations.

We walked along the tree-lined sidewalk for several blocks, passing two, three, and four-story brownstone buildings. It was clear from the start this walk was different from all the other Sunday walks my father and I had enjoyed in the past, when he would proudly share stories about the people he knew who lived in some of those brownstones. This time there was complete silence. Not even the pretty autumn leaves of scarlet and gold I found on the sidewalk and gave to him made a difference in my father's somber mood on that October Sunday in 1949.

We stopped at my father's friend's house. There was no answer when we rang the bell. "It's a nice day; they're probably at the park enjoying the sunshine and will stay there, until the sun goes down. We'll try someone else's house," my father stated with determination. We had no car so we either walked or took buses everywhere. We also couldn't call ahead because we had no telephone. We simply showed up at someone's door, hoping to find the people we wanted to see, at home. Not many families could afford cars, telephones or refrigerators in the late forties—we were among those who couldn't.

Several blocks further we stopped at a place I knew—my aunt's apartment (my mother's sister). She was at home and was glad to see us. My father wasted no time in announcing the reason for our visit, which seemed to surprise my aunt and shocked me because I was not aware of his plan, just as he was not aware of the way I was feeling about his crude approach to my problems in school.

"Could someone in the family help Luba with English?" he asked. My aunt's face took on a red hue and she became silent. I gave my father a disapproving look for putting my elderly aunt on a spot on my account, my aunt who still went to work in spite of her many health problems. When he ignored my obvious displeasure and embarrassment with his gross approach, I expressed my disapproval verbally:

"I wish you had told me why you wanted me to go for a walk with you and visit some friends on the way. If I had known what you were up to, I would have at least tried to talk you out of it, before you went ahead with this embarrassing and uncomfortable idea," I told my father, feeling deceived.

My father put his head down and muttered what was probably not intended for my ears. "That's precisely why I didn't tell you, because I didn't want you to talk me out of it." Then he lifted his head, took off his glasses and, while he cleaned them, said loud and clear what he wanted me to hear. "I do what I do because I love you and want only what's best for you. If you don't understand that now, trust me you will one day." I felt sheepish and wished I hadn't been so quick to judge him, once I realized his intentions were motivated by his love and concern for me, especially when I heard what my aunt had to say.

"Luba, don't be cross with your father; he didn't embarrass me or make me feel uncomfortable, and you and he shouldn't be embarrassed or feel uncomfortable either," she emphasized and went on. "We're family and he brought you to the right place for help, even though, I am sorry to say, I can't help you. You see, I can't read or write English," my aunt confessed and continued. "My job, cleaning offices in New York City most of my life, never required that I know how to read and write English. And there never seemed to be enough time, while working and raising a family of four, to go to school and learn. I always wished I could have helped my own children with school work, when they were growing up and needed help, but I never could, and now I can't help you either, my dear child," my aunt said with all her sincerity and went on. "But I would be glad to ask my children if they could help you, Luba. I'll need a few days, though, since they're all grown up now and on their own, as you know," she genuinely offered.

My father thought a minute and speaking for both of us, he said. "We appreciate your kindness and will check back with you in a few days, if we don't find someone who can start immediately. We're really pressed for time in Luba's case." He then looked at his watch, scratched his head and gestured towards the door, saying, "We must go. Time is marching on and we must too." We both embraced my aunt, placed a kiss on her forehead and said good-bye. Once outside, I walked as fast as I could to keep up with my father's quick stride; his words reverberating in my head, "I do what I do because I love you and want only what's best for you."

We rang the bell in two more houses—other friends of my father's, I presumed—but no one answered. My father seemed upset and I heard him mumble under his breath, "Where are the people when you really need them?" But he was not about to give up and by now, neither was I. "The day is still young and there is plenty of daylight left, so we can see many more people," he reassured me. I asked how many more people he had in mind. "As many as it will be necessary to find someone willing to help you with English," he replied and hurried on.

Before we made another stop, my father explained who the people were. "They're your cousins on my side," he said, as he rang their bell. Luckily, we found the family at home having their late Sunday dinner. All seven of them, including mother and father, seemed to know my father well, and greeted us warmly even though we had interrupted their meal.

Once again, after introducing me to everyone individually, my father wasted no time in announcing the reason for our visit. "Luba needs help with English…" he blurted. I inched my way closer to the door so I could make a quick escape when the excuses and regrets began to pour forth. To my pleasant surprise there were none.

"Every one of us at one time or another wanted to be a teacher, so you've come to the right place, Luba," one of them joshed, and they all laughed heartily recalling that memory in each of their growing-up years. The youngest daughter, Dorothy, lovingly referred to as Dee, was first to volunteer for the job of helping me.

"It's about time I get to play teacher in this house. Everyone else had their turn by practicing on the younger kids in the family, mostly on me. I was always too young—and knew too little—to practice on anyone. That's the price I paid for being born last," she said with a giggle. I relaxed, smiled, and inched my way away from the door, closer to the kitchen table where Dee was sitting.

"Luba, you're welcome to come for help any day of the week. But it has to be after six o'clock in the evening, because I don't get home from the stuffy office until then," Dee stressed.

This must be a dream, I thought. Soon I will wake up and Dee's offer to help will vanish like daylight when night arrives. But Dee meant every word she said, and there was no waking up from a dream because I was not dreaming. I was wide awake when Dee made the offer. And the offer to help was real and as genuine as Dee herself. The days, months, and even years ahead proved that. And it was that moment in time, when Dee offered to share her precious time and knowledge with me, that my life changed for the better again, because my attitude took on a brighter outlook toward everyone in school and everything around me.

The next day in school was unlike any other I experienced before. Everyone in class seemed friendly and kind and the classroom appeared cheery and bright. But why the sudden change all around me? Suddenly it hit me like a bolt of lightning. I bounded into the classroom that morning happy and with a ready smile for everyone. Unlike all other mornings when I walked in with a frozen face, resenting for having to spend time in a gloomy classroom full of unfriendly, foreign-looking kids, when in reality, I was the foreign kid in a class full of natives, and needed to learn their ways in order to be accepted by them and survive in their environment. So, that's what happened! I smiled at the world around me, and this same world smiled back at me. And I had Dee to thank for it, because she opened her heart to me and I, in turn, opened my eyes to new horizons and possibilities in the new to me world. And it all came together because my father loved me enough not to let pride stop him from doing what he felt was necessary to help me succeed.

One afternoon each week our class went to another school, several city blocks of walking distance away, girls for cooking lessons and boys for shop. In the past, I walked on the sidelines by myself, but on the first afternoon after I met Dee I joined the group of giggling girls, with Nina among them, even though I felt strange at first because I didn't understand what the girls were giggling about or if the jokes were on me. But I didn't let that possibility bother me; instead I laughed with them. And when the girls skipped along, I skipped too, even though I felt foolish. I considered myself too mature for such childish behavior but I reasoned, "when in Rome do as the Romans do." And that's what I was doing. At such times I wished I was only fourteen years old like most of my classmates, instead of sixteen, two years older than most of them. I quickly realized, though, this was a senseless wish and a waste of my precious time. My age was not engraved on my forehead, and it was my prerogative to keep it to myself.

That same afternoon in cooking class I participated in cake-making, instead of just observing and tasting, as in the past. I also copied the recipe from the blackboard so I could make the same cake at home. I had a hard time distinguishing where one block of letters ended and another began, and vice versa. But I did the best I could and tucked the recipe in my book to bring home. Dee helped me decipher the recipe and we baked the cake at her house, because as she put it, "we have all the ingredients and utensils here." I proudly carried half the cake home for my father and left the other half for Dee to share with her family.

In all kinds of weather, almost every evening, for the rest of the semester I trudged the several long city blocks to Dee's second floor apartment. Five railroad rooms (a row of rooms without windows except for the first and last room in the row) and a bathroom in the hallway was all there was to her apartment, and it accommodated five siblings (the sixth sibling was married and living in another state), mother, and father. But in spite of its modest appearance, there seemed to be enough love in there to fill a castle. The large kitchen, enhanced by a long and wide table in the center of it, was where the family ate, lived, and entertained on a daily basis. The front room or the parlor was used only on special occasions. The other three rooms were their bedrooms.

Dee always greeted me with a smile and a "Hello there! How are you today?" "What's Miss Sallaro up to these days?" she would ask with a special giggle that endeared her to me even more. And we worked on whatever I needed help with, which was almost everything at first. Dee was only four years older than I and Miss Sallaro had been her teacher, too.

At the end of our half-hour to one hour lesson each day, Dee would never fail to invite me back. "I'll see you tomorrow, and if you should get here before I do, someone else will fill in for me until I get home," she would assure me. And someone always did. Even her dad helped out. Unlike my father, Dee's dad worked a day shift and knew English well, because he was born and educated in America. Dee's mother, on the other hand, spoke only "broken" English and, like my aunt Mary, my mother's sister, and my father, could not read or write English. She too worked in New York City most of her life, cleaning offices at night, so I seldom saw her. But from what I knew of her, one would have had to travel far and wide to find a nicer lady. As time passed, I required less and less help from Dee. But she continued to be there for me much like a baby's security blanket, there for the child if the child needs it. And isn't this a comforting thought?

Nina and I continued walking to and from school each day. We also picked up another friend who lived in the neighborhood and who was in our class—her name was Dana. And since Dana spoke only English, Nina had no choice but to speak English too which was good for me. When my father asked how Nina and I were doing friendship-wise, this is what I had to say:

"I guess we're sort of friends, but the two-year age difference between us and the two different worlds we each grew up in make it difficult for us to understand each other's ways. What Nina considers a funny joke, to me is nothing less than a cruel prank," I told my father.

"Give me an example of a cruel prank," he said.

"Only a few days ago at the end of Nina's visit to our house in the evening, she said good night and I thought she went home, but she really didn't."

"What do you mean? Where did she go?" my father wanted to know.

"Without my noticing, she hid herself in the bathroom, closed the door behind her, opened the bathroom window and climbed out to the fire escape. Out there in the dark, behind the closed kitchen window, she made all sorts of weird noises, which scared me half to death; she even shook the window. I thought for sure we had ghosts in the house, or worse yet, a burglar was trying to break in and I didn't know what to do."

"And did you talk to her about her cruel prank when you found out who it was?" he asked angrily.

"Yes, but Nina didn't think what she did was cruel. She thought what she did was very funny, and I was making too much out of nothing."

"I heard enough. Something has to be done about this," he said, walking away.

"Wait, there is more," I motioned for him to stay put.

"I am positive Nina got my math test to mark the other day in class. We mark each other's test results while Miss Sallaro reads the correct answers. Math is one subject I'm doing well in, so you can imagine how upset I was when I saw a big fat '0' on my test paper. All my correct answers were marked with X's" My father shook his head in disbelief.

"And did you tell your teacher about this? I certainly hope so!" he emphasized

"I showed her the test paper, she checked it over and changed the '0' to '100%.' But she didn't ask who marked my paper and I didn't tell her whom I suspected." My father's face became bright red.

"And why not? What Nina did was downright mean and she shouldn't get away with it. Someone should give her a good talking to and who could be better for the job than her teacher? Would you like me to talk to your teacher?" he wanted to know.

I agreed with my father that Nina should face up to her wrong-doing (if in fact she was guilty), but squealing on her was not the way to go, and I told him so. "I don't want you to get involved—and don't hold a grudge against her either," I pleaded. "If it happens again I promise I will handle it, and in a way that will be good for both of us." Then I decided to tell him something nice Nina had done for me to help him see another side of her:

"Nina can do strange things and some that are downright mean, but Nina herself isn't bad. And maybe our friendship can never be what Pauline and I had, but Pauline isn't here and Nina is. And Nina, too, can be nice and thoughtful at times," I assured him. He motioned for me to explain myself.

"The other day, for instance, Nina insisted I meet a boy who lives next door to her because she thought I might like him. I met John and I do like him. He's not Peter, of course, but his gentle smile and mild manner remind me a lot of Peter. He is also cute and seems as nice as Peter. He is a junior in high school—same school I'll be going to, if I graduate from the eighth grade in January." My father's face broke into a wide smile; he took off his glasses and while he cleaned them, assessed the situation:

"It seems to me you have everything under control. I see no reason why I should get involved, so I won't," he said, and paused before he went on. "Sometimes you have to take the good with the bad as long as the bad doesn't tip the scale below what's normal—I mean where Nina is concerned. I trust you would know if that ever happened. And incidentally, I do know who this young man, John, is. You're a good judge of character and I'm proud of you. I'm also glad you're widening your circle of friends. Nina did a nice thing by introducing you to John," my father admitted. He then patted me on the shoulder and disappeared behind the closed door to his room, presumably to read his newspaper, as always.

"A letter from home! It finally came!" I shouted, when I discovered an envelope in the mail box with familiar handwriting and plastered with foreign postage. I held the envelope in my shaking hands and kissed it several times before I opened it. And I expected so much from such a small piece of paper—six months' worth of wonderful news from home!

"Not a minute passes that we don't think about you. It is now the middle of July (that's when the letter was written and mailed and we received it sometime at the end of October, beginning of November), and still we haven't heard if Luba, arrived safely in America and how both of you are doing." I read the first couple of lines and paused. How could this be? I'd written several letters and my father wrote a few too, and they received none? And it took over three months for this letter to get to us? Then I remembered my father's words. "It's too soon after the war for any kind of normalcy in the world, especially within the foreign postal system..." I continued reading:

"Michael and John were hired out for the season to work for a farmer for food and farm products to bring home. Sometime the farmer gives them some money, too. I am busy at home taking care of the vegetable and flower garden, our three cows and your goat, Luba. Would you believe that little creature never forgot you? We mention your name and she looks around for you...."

Tears flooded my eyes and I couldn't continue reading further. The memories of my family, my friends, my pet goat, the vegetable and flower garden, proved emotionally overwhelming. Suddenly I wished I were back there, living my life with the family I was born into. The long-awaited letter from home didn't do what I expected it to—make me feel better. Once again, I felt so alone, so lonely, and so torn. The petunias on the rooftop that always brightened my cloudy days were now gone. What could I do, who could I turn to, to feel whole again? Then I remembered my mother's parting words: "This is a cloudy day for you but the sun will come out again—it always does. Until then you must make your own sunshine..." I took two quarters out of my Oreo cookie tin, where I kept my rainy-day money, and went downstairs to buy myself an ice cream soda. After I finished my drink, I took a long walk. Was this enough sunshine to chase away the clouds? Not really, but it gave me enough reprieve from the sadness of the moment to finish reading the letter and to get started on my homework.

"We are no closer to going back home than we were two years ago when we were dropped off here. We're here in body but our spirits live mostly in our beloved mountains, which will always be our real home. But can we ever go back? Or is there even anything to go back to? Only God knows for sure at this time. But one way or another we will find out, and soon. Take care of yourselves and remember we love you more than you'll ever know. Your Loving Family."

I placed the letter on the pillow in my father's room, so he could read it when he came home from work after midnight, washed my tear-stained face in cold water and got started on my homework. *I can't afford to slip into the past again. I have too much catching up to do.* I told myself.

The days were short now and getting colder as October turned to November and November to December. The trees let go of their leaves, casting skeletal shadows on the sidewalks. But in spite of the chill in the air, I felt better about myself. Slowly, I was adjusting to life in America and doing much better in school. My vocabulary was increasing daily and I was able to hold limited conversations with Nina and Dana as we walked to and from school every day.

This school day began like any other with Salute to the Flag and reading a verse from the Bible. But for me this day in December of 1949 was different from any other before. In the morning during the Social Studies lesson, Miss Sallaro talked about the atrocities done to humankind by Nazis during the Second World War. I understood enough to know I had a story of my own to tell. Forgetting that my English was still too limited to cover a subject of that magnitude, I raised my hand. And as Miss Sallaro called on me, all eyes in the classroom turned in my direction, since this was the first time I spoke in class in front of all the students.

I was prodded along by Miss Sallaro and a few of my classmates as I told about my brother Michael's hiding place, his capture, and the two years he spent in the Auschwitz concentration camp, until he was liberated at the end of the Second World War. In succeeding lessons I shared other true war stories and experiences. And the more I spoke in class, the less I feared class participation. Several days later I was called into the principal's office. I didn't know what to expect.

"Luba, you will be promoted to high school. You've progressed nicely and we're confident you can handle high school," Miss Robb told me. "It is customary for boys and girls to dress in white on graduation day, even though it's January. Tell your father to buy you a white dress and white shoes, too," she informed me. She then reached across her desk to shake my hand and congratulate me.

This wonderful news was sweet music to my ears, because it showed my efforts were paying off and my life was on the right track. I could hardly wait to share the good news with my father. But I thought the white dress and shoes might be a problem. So when I came home from school that afternoon I counted the change in my Oreo cookie tin. I waited for my father to come home from work after midnight, to tell him the wonderful news. And when I told him about the dress and the shoes I also showed him all the money I had saved for that eventual rainy day—probably enough for the white dress and the white shoes, too.

"Put your money back into the Oreo cookie tin! This is not a rainy day! This is a happy day!" my father proclaimed with a smile. He then opened his wallet and handed me several crisp bills. "Buy yourself the nicest white dress and white shoes you can find," he instructed. I could hardly believe this was my father talking. *Finally, he's gotten over the Great Depression years*, I thought. Or did he part with his money so willingly because he realized my graduation from grammar school and promotion to high school would bring him more happiness than any money in the bank or in his wallet ever could? At any rate, this was a happy moment for both of us. The following Saturday I went shopping for a graduation dress and shoes with Nina and her mother. We bought identical dresses and shoes for this all-important, very special occasion.

On graduation day the auditorium was packed. My father was there sitting as close as he could to the stage. Dee and her parents and my aunt Mary and a couple of her children were there also. The girls in white dresses wearing pink corsages and boys in white suits sporting blue lapel ribbons danced together for the audience.

Before the presentation of diplomas, Miss Robb asked if any graduates would like to do something extra—such as sing or dance— which was not a part of the program. Suddenly, out of nowhere, a scene from another time and place flashed before my eyes. It was at a school concert back in exile, when I was entrusted with a solo and messed up. I suffered stage fright so severe that I couldn't even utter a word, much less sing a solo. When the music teacher got hold of me after the unsuccessful concert, she was literally ready to kill me. She shook me so hard that for a moment I thought she would kill me for sure, so I promised her if she let me go I would not attempt to sing in front of an audience ever again. It was time to break that unreasonable promise, made under great duress. I raised my hand to my own surprise and the surprise of Miss Robb, the graduating class, my father, and the audience.

Almost in defiance, I stood in the center of the stage, as if to say "I can sing in front of an audience!" And I did! I held my head high and let my voice fill the auditorium. When I finished singing—an upbeat Lemko song my brother Michael taught me while in hiding— Miss Robb began to clap and the audience joined in. And when my father stood up, the rest of the people in the audience stood up, too. I could hardly believe that moment was really happening. Not only did I receive my diploma and was officially graduated from grammar school, ready for high school, I also conquered—to some degree—my stage fright. From the corner of my eye I saw my father giving me the "thumbs up" as I shook Miss Robb's hand when she handed me my well-deserved diploma.

Chapter 11

First Day Failures

"*In high school you'll be competing with top-notch students from other* schools...."This excerpt from Miss Robb's farewell speech to the 8A graduating class frightened me when I first heard it, and continued to haunt me. The evening before the start of high school, the sound of those prophetic words resonated in my mind like echoes of some of the worst summer storms back home in the mountains when I was alone in the fields watching over the grazing herd. My English was still so limited, I was not ready to compete with anybody, much less with "top-notch students from other schools." And I didn't see myself entering high school in the same way my smiling and enthusiastic classmates did—who had spent eight years in grammar school (in addition to kindergarten) preparing for it. For me, high school was another frightening unknown for which I felt unprepared, especially as the time drew closer to the opening of schools and for me of high school. If only there was someone or something I could turn to for comfort. I yearned. As usual, I was alone in the apartment because my father was at work, and the radiant summer petunias on the rooftop— my source of inspiration—were now in deep winter sleep, under a heavy blanket of snow.

In desperation I turned to the treasured memories of my Carpathian Mountains. Soon I was back in my ancestral home frolicking in the snow with my best friend, Pauline. Then in the cozy log home warming my cold feet and hands in front of the wood-burning stove, waiting for the hardy supper of potatoes and sauerkraut cooking on top of the stove, with all my family nearby. Suddenly reality hit home and I was back in our third floor apartment, my mind preoccupied with the same fears and doubts as before. Blessedly, the church bells across the street from our apartment began to chime as they did every evening at the same time. The minute I heard this serene melody in the past, it was my signal to let go of troubling thoughts and focus on pleasant ones. This day was no exception. At the first chime, I visualized the petunia garden in bloom again, which gave way to promises of other bright seasons not only for the petunias but also for me. Peace of mind returned at least for a portion of that evening.

Morning was only a few hours away and with the rising sun the first day of the next four years of my life would begin. And it was time to get to bed—to get a good night's sleep and wake up refreshed, ready to face the first day of high school in the morning. But instead of the refreshing sleep I anticipated, I found myself tossing and turning all night long. And I blamed the restless night on the howling winds and crackling ice outside my bedroom window. I even blamed the things that always lulled me to sleep, such as my father's footsteps when he returned home from work after midnight, or his snoring when he settled in his bed and fell into a deep sleep. I was glad when daybreak finally came. But I wished this day was over before it even began, and I was back home from school in our warm and cozy apartment, feeling at ease because all had gone well and confident that all would go well in days and years to come.

To my dismay, nothing seemed to go right for me on the morning of the first day of high school. The kerosene heater quit generating heat because it was empty and the house became ice cold, resembling the frosty weather outside. To solve this problem, I brought up a container of kerosene from the dreaded dungeon-like cellar and rekindled the flame. With the heater working again, I made my breakfast of the usual oatmeal and milk mixture, but this time, the pasty stuff refused to slide down my throat. I didn't understand why I was experiencing those unpleasant feelings again. Especially, since I was sure I had resolved most of them the night before. Then it occurred to me: I had no one to talk to about my feelings of doubts and fears. No one to say good-bye to when I left the house for school. No one to embrace me and wish me good luck. And I left the house angry. Angry with my father that he didn't wake up to see me off; angry with my mother and brothers that they were so far away from me; angry with myself that I was not fluent in English; angry that there was a cruel war which kept us apart, forcing us to live in different parts of the world now.

Nina and I had made plans to meet at her house and walk together to the bus that would take us to school. But when I came to call on her, she was not ready. I found her running in and out of her bedroom—trying on different outfits—while her mother followed in her footsteps collecting what Nina peeled off. When she finally got herself dressed to her satisfaction, to my eyes, she looked more like a model than a student on the first day of high school. I adjusted the collar on my warm coat and made sure the zippers on my lined boots were zipped. The coat and the boots were gifts from my father for which I was most grateful that long-ago, blustery winter morning and thereafter. The rest of my clothes were much-appreciated hand- me-downs (washed and ironed) from my aunt. Nina's mother kissed and hugged Nina tenderly as she shed a few tears. She then placed a kiss on my forehead and we were out the door to a new beginning.

We met Dana at the bus stop and the three of us huddled together to keep warm as we waited for the bus. Half an hour or so later we arrived at our destination. The school was two blocks from where the bus driver let us off. A three-story ornate brick and granite early 20th century building, majestically set on a hilly lot, enhanced by several trees and enclosed by a wrought-iron fence.

We climbed several concrete steps to a huge double door that led to a large vestibule. In the center of it stood an immense bronze statue of Abraham Lincoln, the sixteenth president, for whom the school was named. To the right and left of the statue were steps leading up to second and third floors where most classrooms were located. Directly opposite the statue to the right was a huge auditorium where freshman students were directed for orientation.

"Good morning, Class of January 1954. Welcome to Abraham Lincoln High School—your home away from home for the next four years," echoed the voice of the principal, Dr. Quigley. I felt good that

I had no problem understanding Dr. Quigley's welcoming address. That feeling changed when I felt a poke in my side. "Look at me and listen, I'll tell you what the principal is saying," Nina instructed. Heads began to turn in our direction when I objected.

"I'm doing okay by myself," I said, pulling back in annoyance. But Nina didn't give up. She insisted that I listen to her. Not wanting to create more commotion than we already did, I gave in. But I resented the fact that Nina didn't respect my wishes, even if her intentions were good. I missed my first challenge in high school and I was upset.

"We're meeting here at three," Nina ordered, pointing to the statue of Lincoln as she, Dana, and I separated and went in different directions. All three of us were assigned to different home rooms. "Remember! Three o'clock after school at the statue of Lincoln in case I'm not in any of your classes to remind you," she reiterated. I silently prayed that she was right about not being in any of my classes. As much as I feared facing all the unknowns on the first day of school by myself, I was grateful for the answered prayer—Nina was not in any of my classes. Now I was free to make my own mistakes and learn from them without Nina's stifling protection and offer to help every step of the way, whether I needed it or not.

It cannot be disputed that certain experiences in life stand above all others. Without question, my first day of high school met that criterion. Somehow, I managed to get through the difficult and awful day. And I met Nina and Dana at the statue of Lincoln at three o'clock as Nina instructed. But on the bus going home, the only one who talked non-stop was Nina as Dana listened. As for me, I was too tired to talk and too engrossed in my own thoughts about everything that happened in school. I was glad Nina was not in any of my classes because I didn't have to explain why I handled things the way I did and be told how I should have handled them.

The first day of high school left me exhausted and overwhelmed by so many things: the hugeness of the building; the endless corridors; the infinite rows of classrooms; the complicated and confusing schedules; the pile of books on my aching arm and the many instructions I didn't fully understand. Everything in combination gave me a whopping headache. So when the three of us got off the bus when we reached our destination, all I could think of was to get home as quickly as I could. I wanted to be alone to try to make some sense out of the day's happenings. "See you in the morning," I said to my two companions—and hurried home.

I dropped the books on the table and checked the kerosene heater because the house felt ice cold again. My father must have lowered the flame before he left for work to save the kerosene, and the flame went out, I reasoned. I rekindled the flame and proceeded to make supper for myself. I boiled two eggs, made two pieces of toast, poured myself a glass of milk and ate my supper in my usual place, by the window overlooking the petunias' summer home. When the snowy view of the rooftop disappeared in the darkness of the early winter night, I closed the curtains, turned on the light and began examining the textbooks I brought home from school.

I picked up a book from the top of the pile in front of me and thumbed through its pages. Most words and names—if not all—in that thick history book were unfamiliar to me. I matched the book with the classroom and the teacher and shoved it to the side. Next was an English grammar book with strange-looking words and diagrams drawn here and there throughout the book which baffled my already confused mind. Discouraged, I also shoved it to the side. A ray of hope flashed through my mind when I examined the book of numbers. I can handle this subject, I assured myself. With a hint of a smile, I recalled the classroom and the teacher who said. "If you do well in this class and complete the course, you'll be ready to enter the world of bookkeeping and accounting." Perhaps I should have quit when I was ahead, because the next book I picked up was a shorthand text, a book filled with lines and curlicues which totally crushed my delicate spirit. "To prepare you young ladies for secretarial work," I remembered the teacher telling the class. I couldn't even imagine myself in such a prestigious position as "secretary," and neither could I spell the word "secretary." And there were still other books to examine—geography, social studies—which I decided not to look through. I've had enough for one day!

Even the homeroom presented a challenge I needed to work at. In addition to the daily class recital of the Pledge of Allegiance to the

Flag which I still didn't know verbatim, there was also the reading of the Bible. Following the salute to the Flag the first thing in the morning, the teacher randomly picked a student to read a passage from the Bible. I couldn't see myself standing in front of the class trying to pronounce those difficult words and names from that ancient Book.

And then there was the physical education class in the basement of the building. The teacher, dressed in a dark-blue split skirt, white blouse, and saddle shoes intimidated me by her stern appearance and precise description of her expectations. "I will conduct the exercises for a couple of weeks only," she told the class. "After that I will expect you young ladies to know the routines well enough that if I call on you, you'll be able to conduct the exercises without my help. I will meanwhile be checking each of you for proper postures and to make sure you're doing the exercises correctly," she explained. The possibility that any time after the two-week period I might be called upon to lead the class in exercises put me in a state of panic.

I was frustrated and discouraged. The road ahead appeared much tougher than I even expected. I worried that I would not be able to keep up and fit in with the rest of the students; to live up to the expectations of the straitlaced mostly female teachers, dressed in dark blue and black suits. My fears and doubts continued to grow until my mind created a mountain of reasons why I should feel inferior and different from the rest of the students, a mountain too high to climb in hopes of ever reaching the top. It would be a lot less humiliating and frustrating for me to walk around the imagined gigantic spire with my feet planted firmly on the ground, I thought. But that would mean dropping out of school after the first day. And was this what I really wanted to do? I was still wrestling with my anguished thoughts when I heard the key turning in the door of our apartment. It was after midnight and my father was coming home from work. *Now is my chance to tell him how I feel about everything*, I decided last minute.

"Everything that could go wrong with those damn weaving machines went wrong tonight," my father was saying under his breath as he walked through the door. He then slipped out of his overcoat, kicked off his boots, said good night and closed the door to his room behind him. And he never noticed my sullen face and red eyes or the books strewn all over the table in front of me. He probably didn't even see me sitting there. A few minutes later he stormed out of his room fully awake.

"Why are you still up and not sleeping as you should be? Is there something wrong?" he asked alarmed. And I opened my mouth, ready to blurt out all the wrongs that suddenly moved in on me, including, "I want out of school! Look at all those books and what's expected of me. There is no way I can keep up even with Dee's occasional help." But I noticed how pale and exhausted he looked. So instead of reciting the list of "all the wrongs," I heard myself say: "Nothing's wrong—go to bed and get some rest and I'll do the same." But I vowed that I would wake him up early in the morning and spill out everything that was wrong in my world.

Chapter 12

One Mountain or Four Hills

I jumped out of bed at the sound of the alarm clock and rushed to awaken my father—to tell him I wanted to drop out of high school. I was about to knock on his bedroom door when my eyes caught sight of two packages on the kitchen table boasting radiant bows. My curiosity got the best of me, and I made a spur-of-the-moment decision to check them out before I awakened my father. My attention focused on the larger package, upon which rested an envelope with my name on it. Anxious to find out what was inside the envelope, I tore it open, pulled out a note written in my father's Cyrillic handwriting, and read its contents:

> "I'm sorry I didn't see you off yesterday morning when you left for your first day of high school; or the evening before the first day of school, to give you these presents and to wish you good luck—not only on the first day of high school, but throughout all the days of the next four years. I know, deep down in my heart, you will complete all four years with flying colors and get your high school diploma, because you're not a quitter. Once you set your mind to do something, you see it through, even when the going gets tough. I have no doubt you will do well not only in school but throughout your whole life. And I am sure you will realize your dreams, which are my dreams for you, too!

Your Loving and Proud Father."

The unexpected note and the gifts from my father plunged my decision to leave school into a pit of confusion. *Why is it things always happen when you least expect, and always at the wrong time?* I questioned. Gripped with emotion, I needed to rethink my situation. Should I open the gifts and give school another chance, or return the unopened presents to my father and hope he would understand why I couldn't accept them? I could never live up to his high expectations of me. High school would simply be too hard for me to handle at this late stage in my life—almost seventeen years old and unprepared for such a steep climb.

As curious as I was to find out what was hidden beneath those colorful bows and wrapping paper, I decided to give the gifts back to my father, unopened. It was for the best, I reasoned. Yet, the something or someone that made me notice the gifts in the first place nudged me also to take a peek at what was inside those decorated boxes.

I opened the bigger box first. In it I found luscious-looking dark chocolates filled with fruits and nuts smiling at me in defiance; the irresistible kind worth dying for. But I resisted the temptation; the peek satisfied my curiosity for the moment. I closed the box, taped the wrapping paper in place, and placed it on the table where I found it. My downfall came when I peeked at the contents in the smaller box. The lovely pen and pencil set inscribed with the words, "To Luba—From Her Proud Dad," on the side of the fountain pen, and, "God Bless, Luba," on the side of the mechanical pencil. Unlike the box of chocolates, I could not close the box with the pen and pencil set after a peek.

This special gift seemed packed with love from someone who loved me most—my father—and asked nothing in return except to follow my dreams through education. How could I deny him this or myself? *How dare I entertain thoughts of dropping out of high school after only one day, or ever!* I chastised myself. Maybe the loving note and the special gifts from my father came at exactly the right time, inspired by a divine being who loved me and wanted the very best for me—like my father. Perplexed and exhausted from the emotional roller coaster, I rested my head on the kitchen table—next to all my school books, the note and the gifts—to do some serious thinking about what had transpired, but mainly about my earlier decision to quit school. Suddenly, a gentle voice like that of an angel interrupted my thoughts:

"Yes, you can do well in school—your father is right. Give yourself a chance—you deserve it. School will not be easy at first and there'll be a lot you won't understand so don't expect to rise to the top too quickly, because you'll become so overwhelmed with everything that in the end you'll do nothing. And don't compare yourself to other students in school. Remember, you have almost seventeen years of catching up to do—most of your classmates haven't even lived that long! Trod slowly but steadily and you will get to your destination—trust me…."

"All good and well, but—" I heard myself say before I was interrupted by the same "someone or something:"

"No but! Please listen—I'm not finished," the loving voice continued. "Stop worrying so much and jumping way ahead of yourself. I don't know if you're aware you've created a mountain out of molehills, or should I say layers of fear, inferiority, inadequacies, and differences in your case? Now the mountain is too steep to climb, the goals impossible to reach, and the only way out of this mess is to quit everything—high school after only one day! True, the work may be overwhelming at first, but you're a survivor—you've survived worse. When you were born, for instance, no one expected you to live and no one intervened on your behalf, and yet you lived; when the bombs dropped and you were caught in the line of fire, the odds for survival were stacked against you, yet you survived; when you were pushed by a playmate from the hay loft and headed straight for the cement floor below, you landed atop another stack of hay, instead of the cement floor where you should have; when you found yourself immersed in human waste to the tips of your earlobes you climbed out of the outhouse and survived the mess; when a wagon pulled by four horses came upon you, riding your bicycle to school and the driver looked for you under the wagon, he found you untouched on the side in lush grass…. You're meant to live and expected to leave your 'heart' prints behind! But that can only happen through education in your case. Do you see the picture?" the unseen being, seemingly speaking from the depth of his or her heart, wanted to know.

"I'm not sure I do," I heard myself answer so the gentle voice went on:

"Divide the mountain into four hills—that's how many years it will take you to complete the high school courses you're so over-whelmed by. Remove the fear, the inferiority, the inadequacy; you don't deserve any of them. Keep the differences—being different is being unique, and that's good. Remember, what makes us different from one another is not as important as what makes us alike. Anyway, it would be a dull world if the people in it were all the same. Don't you agree? Now look up at your mountain. What do you see?" the unseen being asked.

"I see four hills; the mountain is gone," I answered.

"Precisely," the kindly voice agreed and still went on. "Now with some effort you'll be able to walk up each hill—slowly, one step at a time—while enjoying the view around you and finally from the top of each hill. And remember to look for some special flowers, a little dif-ferent from the ones that usually grow in the area, like you."

"I should have no problem walking up these hills—one hill at a time. I was born and raised in the hills. Thank you for taking time to talk to me and showing me the way," I said to the unseen being. Then I picked up my head from the table, opened my eyes and looked around. There was no one in the room and no other sound besides the clock on the wall ticking away seconds and minutes—rhythmically—and my father's peaceful snoring. Had I been dreaming?

I dressed myself quickly, grabbed a piece of bread and a few pieces of chocolates from my gift box, and was out the door with all my books, leaving my father to snore in his room, undisturbed. It was get-ting late and I had to hurry if I wanted to make the bus. And I almost missed it, but Nina and Dana saw me running in the distance and asked the bus driver to wait for me.

"You're late—did you oversleep?" Nina wanted to know as I climbed the steps of the bus.

"I'm not sure if I overslept and I'd rather not talk about it. What matters is that I'm here and hopefully I will be on time from now on."

I told Nina. I knew she would not understand what really took place. How could she, or anyone else for that matter, if I myself didn't understand. What I knew for sure was that the experience with the unseen being changed my attitude towards everything around me, for which I was grateful.

As soon as we settled in our seats on the bus we heard from Nina.

"My College Prep course is much harder than your Commercial course, Luba, and even your General course, Dana," she informed us.

"Luba, I hope you realize you can never go to college with your business subjects but I'm college-bound with my College Prep ones," she boasted.

"The best you'll be able to do is to get a job in some stuffy office taking orders from someone else—that's if you ever graduate from high school. I can be a teacher or maybe even a college professor," Nina prophesied. Then Dana spoke:

"Since you seem to be able to predict the future, can you tell me mine?" Dana asked Nina and smirked at me which Nina saw. Nina's feelings became hurt and she stopped talking. I wondered how long her silence would last. She was seldom lost for words. But on this second day of high school—following my earlier experience with the gentle voice—innuendoes thrown in my direction that I was different and inferior to everyone else no longer had the power to undermine my spirit as it had in the past. I knew where I was going and how I was going to get there.

"I guess we're stuck with being locker room neighbors for the next four years," Nina joshed as Dana and I opened our lockers next to hers. Nina quickly forgot she was not on speaking terms with us.

"Neighbors at home and neighbors in locker room—double pleasure or double trouble," Dana added and the three of us laughed. *That's how friends should behave*, a thought crossed my mind. After all, we were friends in spite of our differences.

I hung up my coat, dropped off the books I didn't need for morning classes, and hurried to my homeroom. Half-way up the stairs I heard Nina holler.

"See you in lunchroom at noon."

"I'll be there," I yelled back and became lost in the crowd.

I followed my schedule and jotted down, to the best of my ability, what I thought was important about each class, and in a separate section of the notebook my homework for each subject. And there was a lot of homework at the end of that second day in school and in the days, weeks, and months that followed. Also a lot I didn't understand, which often frustrated me to the depth of my being. But the words of wisdom from the unseen being—"Trod slowly but steadily. Don't give up,"—kept me at a safe distance from the abyss of despair I found myself in after that overwhelming first day in school when I was ready to quit high school. That evening I revisited Dee. And I did that every time I needed help, for the rest of the first semester of high school— Spring 1950—and semesters that followed.

"I'm glad to see you, Luba. Tell me about high school—my alma mater," Dee said when she saw me again.

And we talked about school, but mostly we worked on things I needed help with. Some things like bookkeeping I was able to do by myself, so we shoved that homework to the side. But Oh! how grateful I was for Dee's help with other subjects, such as Greek Mythology which was part of English. I had enough trouble making sense of simple English words; adding Old English ones was like asking me to learn another foreign language. Dee managed to break the weird-sounding mythological expressions into simple English sentences which I could understand, and she was patient enough to continue doing it until I caught on to the strange-sounding phraseology—in that subject as well as others.

On another level, I realized the distance I still had to tread before I reached the plateau of fluency in English equal to my classmates when at the beginning of the first semester, I was given an Intelligence Test along with the rest of the freshman class to determine our academic standing in relation to students from other schools. While my classmates seemed to have no difficulty and breezed through the multiple-choice exam, I found it extremely difficult.

Most of the multiple-choice questions, and there were over a hundred of them, consisted of expressions and figures of speech I was not familiar with, and I guessed every answer. For example: "When used in a sentence what does the phrase mean? (choose a, b, c or d): Give someone a cold shoulder; give someone the third degree; wild goose chase; strike while the iron is hot; egg someone on...." In every case I opted for the literal meaning of the phrase or the one closest to it, and in each case the answer was wrong. A few math problems seemed easy, but even those I figured incorrectly because the questions were tricky and misleading, and I was not sophisticated enough in English to pick it up.

As time passed, I learned about the various American/English expressions and figures of speech, the metaphors and the analogies as well as the homonyms and the homophones, and their applications in the written/spoken language. And I wished I could have taken that wretched Intelligence Test over again, because I realized where I went wrong and I dreaded to find out how badly I must have done on it. I even inquired about an exception in my case and to be allowed to take the test over, but was denied. *It's water under the bridge*, I thought as I recalled one of the phrases on the test.

It was a sad day for me when the results of the Intelligence Test came back. At the top of mine, written in bold red letters, I saw the following: "Very Poor—Low IQ—Equivalent to an Imbecile." That day I came home from school completely devastated. While other students—including Nina and Dana—bragged about their test results in school and on the way home, I had mine hidden in between the pages of the thickest book, which happened to be the United States history text. At home I let go of the suppressed tears, but not of my homework and additional work I usually did on my own, such as learning at least ten new words each evening. I was more determined than ever to master the finer points of the English language as well as its diversified usage, now that I was aware of it. I read aloud to myself; I listened intently when others spoke; I talked to myself when I was alone, which was most of the time; I drilled myself in spelling, which at first I found very difficult. And when I ran into trouble, I ran to Dee's house for help.

Often I studied late into the night and stopped when I heard my father's footsteps on the first floor when he came home from his night shift job after midnight. By the time he reached our third floor apartment, I had all the lights turned off and pretended to be fast asleep.

This way he never had to worry I wasn't getting enough sleep or using electricity unnecessarily. But this night I purposely waited for him because I needed a shoulder to cry on, even though I wasn't sure telling him how upset I was about my Intelligence Test results was a good idea. But he was the only one I could share my pain with and so I took a chance. He didn't react very well to the grade on my test papers—much worse than I expected or imagined:

"I'm going to school with you in the morning and give those foolish teachers a piece of my mind. Giving you such a test when your English is still so limited is absurd. I'll tell them a thing or two that will open their eyes as well as their ears," my father threatened, his face bright red and fire in his eyes.

"No! No! you can't do that," I begged. "If the students see you coming to school with me, everyone will know something is very wrong, especially Nina. And if she finds out about that hideous word on my test paper, "Imbecile, (and she has her ways) she'll never let me forget it. In a joking way, she'll taunt me forever. But to me this is no laughing matter. I want to forget I ever took that test. As far as I'm concerned it never happened and I was never stigmatized in such an ugly way. And it will not stop me from learning as quickly and as much as I can, to prove to everyone just how intelligent I am," I assured my father. He listened intently, and when I finished my spiel he had a few chosen words of his own to add:

"That-a-girl, Luba, show them—I know you can do it. I never had any doubt about your intelligence and ability to do well in whatever you choose to do, including high school. Remember, this test is not a measure of your intelligence or ability—it means nothing in your case, because it should never have been given to you in the first place." With that, the redness on my father's face and the fire in his eyes began to fade, and I too felt much better. I got everything off my chest and was ready to put this day to rest, so I, as well as my father, could get much needed rest, too. I thanked him for listening to me and said good night—morning was only a few hours away and another busy day was waiting for me.

It took a couple of months into the first semester of high school before I mustered enough courage to raise my hand in class to answer a question. It happened the first time in biology class. I knew the answer to an experiment and raised my hand. I didn't know some of the scientific words needed to explain the process and found myself in trouble. I was ready to give up in the middle of the explanation because I heard snickers from some classmates, but the dear old white-haired teacher, whose name I have since forgotten but not her sympathetic nature, jumped to my rescue. She supplied the necessary words and saved me from myself. With her help, everyone in class seemed to understand the process of the experiment, but I'm not sure anyone truly understood what I had accomplished that day in the biology class. The teacher thanked me for a job well done and before I left for the next class she spoke to me privately:

"Luba, I didn't realize English was not your language. I want you to know I admire you for your courage in class today—keep up the good work. Also, feel free to come to me for help should you need it," she offered. Her words of praise and encouragement, together with my own accomplishment in her class that day, laid the first cornerstone in the foundation on which all my future successes in high school rested.

One morning I awakened early because the chirping birds outside my window wouldn't let me sleep. I looked out to see what the clamor was all about and was surprised that the snow on the surrounding rooftops, as well as on the roof where colorful petunias had bloomed last summer, was gone. And the lone scrawny tree below my window, squeezed in between the weather-beaten buildings and ravaged by winter's fury, showed signs of life again. It was springtime and I didn't even realize it. I was too busy keeping up with my school work to notice that the season of darkness was moving out and the season of light was moving in—not only in nature but in my life as well. Hard work in school and at home was finally paying off!

The history lesson that long-ago spring day in 1950 brought back memories of the Second World War which I desperately wanted to forget, especially those that were still causing me nightmares. Now some of the worst ones resurfaced and begged to be shared with the rest of the class. Several times I half-raised my hand to speak and each time I lost courage and quickly lowered my hand. I was afraid my classmates would make fun of my still-awkward English. When I could no longer suppress the urge, I raised my hand again. This time it stayed up until I was asked to speak.

To my surprise and delight there were no snickers or giggles when I spoke, as I expected. The classroom became quiet and everyone listened intently as I told about my brother Michael's hiding place to avoid the Nazi concentration camp. It was my job, I told the class, to watch out for the Gestapo, and when they appeared in the village, which happened frequently, to run home as fast as my legs could carry me to warn Michael and help him hide. I told about one occasion when a Nazi soldier actually sat on top of the ancient trunk that covered the hole in the floor where my brother was hiding, put me on his knee and gave me candy so I would tell him about Michael's whereabouts. I told the class about the consequences that awaited our whole family if Michael was found—instant execution by the same Gestapo who found him. Fortunately, I understood what was facing us even though I was very young, and convinced the Nazis—tears flowing down my cheeks—I had no idea where Michael was. Finally, I told the class how Michael was captured—on the train on the way to another hiding place—and sent to Auschwitz Concentration Camp, where he spent two horrific years until he was liberated along with other survivors when the Second World War ended in 1945.

A girl sitting next to me began to cry when she heard "Auschwitz Concentration Camp." She sadly revealed to the class her grandparents died there. And she must have seen a connection between us, because from that day on her indifference towards me turned to friendship. Other classmates wanted to hear more about my war experiences. I promised to talk about them when the subject in history class came up again. I was no longer afraid to participate in that class, either. The barrier between me and my classmates in history class melted away just like in biology.

My heart skipped several beats when the homeroom teacher called on me one morning, shortly after I shared my war experiences in history class. I was not ready yet to read from the ancient book— the Holy Bible—and that's what I thought she wanted me to do. I panicked!

"Luba, Dr. Quigley wants to see you. Take the excuse slip and go to his office," she ordered. My legs and hands shaking, my mind paralyzed by fear, I entered Dr. Quigley's office. I expected to hear some tragic news.

"Luba, I hear interesting things about you from your teachers and classmates," Dr. Quigley said. I breathed a sigh of relief but still I waited to hear the rest of the reason why I was summoned to the principal's office before I let myself relax. Surely, he had more important things to do than to chat with me about what my teachers and classmates are saying about me, whatever that was, I reasoned.

"Your history teacher told me...and I was wondering if you wouldn't mind sharing some of your war experiences with the rest of us in school during an assembly one day?" Dr. Quigley asked. My first impulse was to say "No" and make a quick exit out of his office on a pretense I didn't want to be late for my first morning class. But the diplomas and testimonials in fancy frames which decorated the walls of his office impressed me, and I changed my mind.

"Yes, I will do it," I told him. I wanted at least one diploma of my own and I would never get it if I continued being afraid. Anyway, the gentle voice on the second day of school, when I was ready to quit high school, had told me fear didn't belong in my life.

Dr. Quigley retired shortly after our conversation because of ill health, and the new principal, Dr. Coyle, had his own way of handling things. He made up a list of questions and met with me one day so I could answer them. At the beginning of the assembly on the day of the presentation, he introduced me to the assemblage before he read my answers to his questions. At the end of the presentation, he asked the students in the assembly if they had any questions to ask me. And there were a few questions which I no longer remember, nor do I remember how I answered them. But I do remember receiving a standing ovation at the end, which made my spirit soar almost to the top of my first hill—immersed in bright spring sunshine.

Chapter 13

Disturbing News from Home

The smile my father sported when he left the house to do our weekly grocery shopping, this long-ago late spring in 1950, was now gone. The stooped-over figure, pale gray face, absence of spring in his stride, and subdued manner, were not my father's usual characteristics. Knowing him as well as I did by this time, I knew something serious—or at best unexpected—must have occurred between the time he left the house and his return. But what? I wondered. Especially when he dropped off the half-full grocery bags on the kitchen table and didn't bother to unpack them as he always did. Nor did he boast about the money he had saved by comparison shopping, which would be put away for that "rainy day" engraved in his mind with an indelible ink. He was about to slam the door behind him to his bedroom when I stopped him and questioned his weird behavior:

"Is something wrong?" I earnestly but fearfully asked. When he hesitated to answer my question, I asked again.

"You're very upset! Please tell me why!" With head bowed low, he reluctantly pulled out a letter from his pocket which was plastered with foreign postage. He then asked me to sit down. It was obvious the letter was from home, but what news it brought was still unknown to me. Judging from my father's somber look, I feared the worst, but how I was going to deal with it, I didn't know.

"Did something bad happen back home? Tell me—I want to know the truth no matter how painful!" I asked in desperation, frightened half to death because in reality that's what my mind perceived—death of one of my loved ones back home. Especially after I heard my father whisper in a barely audible voice. "We received disturbing news from home." Death was no stranger to me. It had touched many lives of people close to me in my short life. Fortunately by God's grace to date, I had been spared the agony of losing one of my loved ones—the worst loss of all. Both sets of my grandparents, as well as a baby sister, had died before I was born. The phrase, "to have known them was to have loved them," would have been a fitting epitaph for each of them. But when fate denied me the honor and joy of knowing them, it also spared me the grief of losing them. Had I reached the end of death-free journey of a loved one? Must I now face death, face-to-face? *Please God, give me strength to endure what I cannot change!* I prayed silently.

As a young girl of about six, I remember standing in the corner of the neighbor's house sobbing, because a little boy I had played with the day before, was dying. The child's mother and grandmother hovered over little Peter, praying out loud, while water on the wood stove was warming to wash his dead body. That's how certain they were of his imminent death, since there was no one in the village, and nothing on earth, to intervene in his untimely demise at that moment.

I witnessed with much sadness many funeral processions passing our house. The men carrying open caskets to church—accompanied by banner-bearers depicting venerated saints and martyrs—for farewell services and then to the cemetery next to the church for burials, while wailing family members, young and old villagers, followed. I lived through countless such heart-wrenching scenes—more than my share in the fourteen years I lived there. That's probably why I equated "disturbing news from home" and tears in my father's eyes with the death of a loved one.

Growing up, I knew families with many children, but only two or three survived and lived to adulthood. Also households with orphans, because the mothers died in childbirth or fathers at an early age. I remember one house in our neighborhood completely devoid of people, because the entire family was wiped out during a plague that invaded the village in the early part of the twentieth century. But so far my mother and brothers, the family I left behind, and of course the father I lived with now were all alive and well. Or were they? Finally, I asked my father a point-blank question!

"Did my mother die, or did something horrible happen to Michael or John?" I mustered enough courage to ask, my hands and legs shaking uncontrollably.

My father must have seen the unduly emotional state this "disturbing news from home" left me with. He put his hand on my shoulder and even tried to smile, as he spoke: "Calm down," I faintly heard him say. "Your mother and brothers are alive and well."

"They are? Then the news from home can't be as bad as you made it out to be," I reprimanded him as I breathed a sigh of relief.

"Here's the letter; judge for yourself," he said as he handed it to me, his hands still trembling. "Read it out loud and slowly, so I can hear every word clearly," he requested. Maybe I didn't understand everything, but I think I did," he credited himself. I took the letter and began to read as he asked but deep down I wished I could have read it silently, because my voice was still trembly.

"I made a trip back home to the mountains," my mother wrote in her self-taught Cyrillic writing (Lemko-Rusyn) which probably only my father and I could decipher correctly. "It was a long and difficult journey! Many hours on the rickety old train and then on foot through the pathless mountains, to what I thought was still our village and our home. Foolishly, I expected to find everything the way we left it when we were forced out of our home on that tragic day in July of 1947," my mother said, and went on.

"You can imagine my shock when I found the village overgrown with brush and young trees where most homes had stood. And a pile of manure on the site of our beloved home and our two majestic oak trees. There is no trace that anyone ever lived on that spot." The last two sentences literally took my breath away. I felt weak and my voice faded to an inaudible whisper. I needed time out for composure before I could continue to read on. I excused myself and went to my room. It took several minutes of rest and deep breathing before I could come back to the table and continue reading my mother's profound letter. When I returned, I found my father as I left him—deep in thought and seemingly far removed from the present. Probably not even aware of my temporary absence. I continued to read, this time looking for a glimpse of good news somewhere in the letter, but there was none as far as I could see.

"All our hard work gone with the wind," Mother mournfully informed us. "We truly lost everything we worked for over the years and our ancestors over many centuries. We can never go back because there is nothing to go back to. And even if there was, I found out no one is allowed to return at this time or any time soon—If ever," my mother wrote and then added: "Our land is infested with snakes and it's even dangerous to walk on it, and the same is true throughout the entire Lemkovyna, I heard." And there was still more to read. But again, a lump in my throat and mist over my eyes made it difficult to go on, especially when I read about the snakes. I took another brief respite in my room, which probably my father never noticed, again.

Only once during my entire fourteen years living in the Carpathian Mountains did I encounter a snake. It was while I was mushroom-picking. I picked up a branch of an evergreen tree resting on the moist patch of peat moss where mushrooms usually grew, and there it was. A huge snake! Its skin was reddish in color and its mouth was open ready to attack, I was sure! I dropped my half-full basket of mushrooms picked elsewhere in the forest, and homeward I ran as fast as my skinny legs could carry me—never looking back for fear the snake was on my heels. Breathless, I made it home! I slammed the door to our house behind me and locked it, grateful to be within the walls of its safety, but not sure if the snake was not waiting for me on the other side of the door. Of course it wasn't, I soon realized.

"The snake was not about to leave the safety of his home in the forest and slither all the way to your home after you, Luba," Mother assured me, when I cried on her shoulder as I related this frightening incident to her. "You probably scared the poor thing as much as he scared you. And he was as glad as you were when you parted company," Mother said, as she tried to make light of the situation for my sake. But all her efforts were in vain. To this day, I am deathly afraid of all snakes! Seeing a snake, even under controlled conditions, brings me back to my youth when that incident with the snake happened, and I run from the creature almost as fast as I did then.

In retrospect, the dreadful news from my mother about the demise of our much-loved homestead in the Carpathian Mountains brought back memories of the events which led to the tragedy Mother wrote about—the forced evacuation and confiscation of the Lemko homes and lands:

Once again I heard screams and wailing as soldiers shouted. "You have exactly two hours in which to collect your belongings—no more than you're able to carry on your backs—and be ready to leave your home!" Once again I experienced the oppressive heat in the filthy, disease-infested, windowless car we shared with our three cows on the freight train as we traveled to an unknown destination. Once again we were dropped off on a strange land without a roof over our heads. This was indeed very "disturbing news from home," but still I was grateful because my worst fears were not realized. We were all alive and well!

My year-end report card showed all passing grades. I passed every subject—not with flying colors, but with passing grades, thanks to my hard work, unwavering determination to succeed, and much-appreciated help from Dee! How glad I was now that I didn't give up when on occasions my life dipped to very low points, creating fertile grounds for giving up. Especially when I read the rest of my mother's letter:

"Luba. I know your dream was always to come back to our home in the mountains. I wish I could make your dream come true, but as you can see, I can't. No one can. What we had there is now gone! I hope you are adjusting to your new life in America, and I pray America will always be your 'Home Sweet Home' and also ours, one day. Maybe someday you'll visit the mountains and the place you once called home. This way you can see for yourself the devastation and desecration that took place there."

Mother then signed off the letter, and I was glad there was no more to read. I was disturbed enough, and so was my father, by this "Disturbing News from Home."

Chapter 14

Discovering New Horizons

Besides shock, my father's initial reaction to the "disturbing news from home" was denial, since he had not experienced the painful reality of the forced evacuation in summer of 1947 as I did. Over time, I managed to work through many adverse emotions of that unfathomable ordeal, but not my father. While the unexpected "disturbing news from home" surprised me and left me temporarily stunned, it devastated him—almost to the point of no return. I understood my father's pain because—on some spiritual level—his pain was my pain too. And I soon realized we needed each other if we were to resolve anything and put things in perspective so the healing process could begin, especially for my father, before resentments or regrets took root and further complicated our lives.

My father arose with the rising sun that long-ago Sunday, and made sure I was up too. "The news we received from home yesterday kept me awake most of the night. I need to talk to you," he said with tears in his eyes. While preparing our usual Sunday breakfast of oatmeal, eggs, toast, and tea, we discussed general subjects. During the meal, our conversation turned to reminiscing about our mutual homestead—as I hoped it would. This was my chance to show my father that—difficult as it may seem in the midst of turmoil—every cloud does have a silver lining, but it is up to each of us to find it and make the best of it. I wanted him to know that I believed I had not only found silver linings beneath many threatening dark clouds in my life, but also beautiful rainbows after the furious rain storms the dark clouds brought. I had to show my father it would be a double tragedy if we forever mourned the end of something and failed to celebrate the beginning of another something, such as a glorious spring after a fierce winter back home, and now our life in America because we lost everything back in the Carpathian Mountains.

"Did you know I bought more than half the land and forest that we owned back home? The rest was the inheritance from my parents—your grandparents. Yeah, I bought it with blood, sweat, and tears, and now everything is gone," my father lamented. I handed him a glass of water, being careful not to interrupt his train of thought. As long as he was talking, he was taking steps towards healing, and I was there to lead him on. While sipping the water, he went on:

"And did you know I grew the apple and pear trees in the orchard from seeds, found a young cherry tree growing in the forest and planted it on the hill above the orchard?" he boasted and continued to reminisce. "I will never forget how happy I was when the seedlings began to push through the soil in the flower pots where I buried them," he recalled, cleaned his fogged-up glasses and went on. "When they grew some, I transplanted the saplings to larger containers to give them room to spread their young roots and branches. I gave them lots of love and tender care and they grew to beautiful fruit-bearing trees in the orchard of my pride and joy. I wonder if they're still there or gone with the wind like everything else," my father sighed and paused to contemplate further on his losses.

My father's reminiscences brought back treasured memories of my own, which I shared with him. I remembered the happy time of my childhood when Pauline and I ran barefoot in the lush emerald grass every spring; when the whole world appeared in bloom every May about the time the apple and pear trees in my father's orchard unfurled their delicate pink and white petals and tender green leaves; when Pauline and I picked yellow buttercups and purple violets in the meadows and strung wild strawberries on tall stringy grasses to bring home to our mothers; when we felt light enough to fly with the birds that chirped above our heads. Today I wonder: Was the world around us truly that spellbound and full of wonder, or did it only seemed because we were so young and carefree, and would any place on earth have appeared just as wondrous to our youthful eyes at that magical time of our lives?.

And how could I ever forget the grand old cherry tree on the hill? It was on that hill that my father was going to build us a new, bigger, and better house when he returned from America, after he earned enough money. I remember my mother repeating that promise to us when hopes of surviving the long years of war were waning. How well I remember sitting in the loft of our humble log home, where my great-grandfather, grandfather, father, and I, as well as my siblings, were born, wondering how I would feel when the beloved home was no longer there? What emotions would surface seeing it come down, because supposedly it had outlived its usefulness (not in my mind) and a newer, bigger, and better model was waiting to replace it on another lot of our land—the one above my father's beautiful orchard, and the cherry tree which graced the land around it. Fate had spared me that pain, and now that our ancestral home was gone, I didn't know whether I should be grateful because I was spared the grief of seeing its destruction, or resentful because I was denied its mourning. Neither would have served any purpose, I told my father. The past belongs to the past, but it doesn't mean that it should be forgotten. And so, I would always remember my homestead the way I left it with reverence, and treasure the memories of it for as long as I lived, yet live my life to the fullest in the present wherever that may be! My father listened, and when he thought I was finished, but I wasn't, a faint smile crossed his face.

To make light of the stressful news from home that seemed powerful enough to crush the essence of my father's being, I shared an interesting tidbit from my childhood I thought would amuse him. The incident involved the grand old cherry tree on the hill. I remembered clearly its cascading branches heavy with red juicy cherries which appeared every June or beginning of July. Unfortunately, I was always too short to reach the luscious-looking fruit from the ground and too young to climb the tree by myself. On one occasion I asked my brother John for help, and he obliged; to my later regret. John helped me to climb the cherry tree as far up as I was able to go, told me to eat all the cherries within my reach, and promised to be back to help me down after he completed his chores at home. Soon he disappeared and I was left almost at the top of the tree by myself.

For a time, I was happy because there was an abundance of plump juicy cherries for me to eat. When I realized John was not coming back as he promised I began to cry for help but no one came to my rescue because no one heard me, and I was too frightened to attempt the downward spiral by myself. I felt abandoned and thought I would have to spend the night on the limb of the cherry tree. Luckily my presence at the supper table that evening was missed and mother questioned John about my absence. He finally remembered he left me atop the cherry tree and ran out to get me. He found me safe but very frightened and very upset—needless to say very angry with John.

I don't know exactly how long I had been stuck in that cherry tree or the amount of cherries I ate. I do know the sun was high up in the sky when John helped me climb the tree. When he came back to get me, the sun was gone and the moon was high up in the sky—an eternity for any child. "I will never eat another cherry and never ask John to help me climb another cherry tree," I promised Mother when I came home. But I broke that promise as soon as my stomachache went away and John gave me his solemn promise he would never leave me high up in any tree again—surprisingly he never did. Perhaps because he received punishment from Mother for being negligent— no cherries for him for the rest of the season. Was this a just punishment? I thought so.

"How old were you when this happened?" my father asked. He seemed to have forgotten—at least for the moment—the "disturbing news from home."

"I was no more than six or seven years old, but the memory of that episode is as clear as if I were a child stuck on that cherry tree today," I told him. Suddenly my father's eyes brightened and a wide smile flashed across his face:

"I'm really surprised you would remember that incident with such clarity, since you were still so young when it happened—thanks for telling it to me. Hearing this story makes me feel a lot better about everything that happened back home, because I don't feel as if everything I worked for, and still feel very close to, is completely gone—

not as long as I can hold on to my memories of everything back home like you do," my father said, his eyes open wide as if suddenly he discovered new horizons.

"Not only do I remember the cherry tree, I can still taste the cherries it gave us," I told my father. "I can also taste the juicy apples and pears from the trees you planted in the orchard below it. And I remember so much more about my life there. I'd be glad to tell you all that I remember, if you care to listen some more. You see, all I have to do is close my eyes and the years unfold before me like pages in a book— one by one—as I lived them back there." Then I managed to subtly add what l was leading to all along, hoping it would help my father in his hour of need: "I believe that everything changes with time, and it must, but nothing is ever lost as long as we keep it alive in our memory and pass it on to others as we travel through life." My father thought about what I had said for a minute or so before he spoke:

"Come to think of it, if I close my eyes and choose to go back home in thought, I too, see everything the way it was at different stages in my life—even as far back as my own childhood," my father admitted, and went on; "At that moment I do feel I am back home again, plowing the fields in springtime and planting seeds in the dark, soft soil; harvesting the bounty from the earth in golden autumn, and thanking the Almighty for His Blessings," my father admitted. He seemed in control of his emotions once again and much more accepting of the fate he could not change. And oh! so grateful for the memories of his beloved homestead in the Carpathian Mountains, which no one could take away from him because he had them buried in the deepest part of his heart, where only he had access to them. I knew I had my father back—from the pit of depression when he asked me to go uptown with him because he wanted to treat me to something special. I wasted no time! I wanted to be out the door in case he changed his mind because he remembered the "disturbing news from home" again.

I had heard Nina and Dana mention "pizza pie parlor" on several occasions in the past, but I had no idea where it was or what pizza pie tasted like. But that's where my father took me for that special treat— the pizza parlor on Newark Avenue—the shopping Mecca in my eyes. After we ate the pizza, he ordered his favorite food—the raw clams on half shells. Ironically, I didn't only enjoy the cheese pizza, but also the slimy live creatures from the ocean I had vowed never to eat when I first came to America.

In the spirit of friendship and bonding, I decided to taste one of my father's clams. Without warning, the entire slippery critter, smothered in lemon juice, slid into my mouth. To my surprise this weird creature left a rather pleasant taste. The second and third clams tasted even better. This unexpected sight—me eating raw clams—amused and delighted my father, which in turn helped drive away the somber thoughts and emotions the "disturbing news from home" created.

For the rest of the summer and fall of 1950 and thereafter, almost every Saturday or Sunday afternoon, my father and I walked to Newark Avenue side by side to enjoy our favorite foods: pizza and, of course, clams on half shells smothered in fresh-squeezed lemon juice. On the way to the pizza and clam shanty, we talked and reminisced about everything under the sun, making new precious memories equal to those we now treasured of our never-to-be-forgotten homestead in the Carpathian Mountains.

Chapter 15

My First Job

Growing up in a home rich in traditions, love, and history, amidst acres of food-producing fields and vast forests boasting tall trees suitable for building material or firewood to keep us warm in winter, kept me content and happy—most of the time. I never felt shortchanged or deprived because I had no money. Everything I needed or wanted came from our own plentiful land. We sowed the seeds and planted the seedlings in spring, tenderly cared for them in the summer, harvested the results of our labor in the autumn, and stored everything either in the root cellar or barn to be used when the fields lay dormant under a heavy blanket of snow. In reality, money in my pocket would have served no purpose in those days because there was nothing in our village of Liszczyny I could buy for it, since there were no stores of any kind where money could be exchanged for something nice or good.

I soon realized life in America was as different from the one I was used to as day is from night. In America you need money to live—especially people like us, living in an apartment without a speck of land to plant a seedling upon. But did we really need the land to live a good life in America? Not really, I soon found out—not as long as you brought home a check at the end of each week or month. And that's what I wanted to do that long-ago summer of 1950—taste life outside my home and the classroom and get paid for it.

At seventeen and in high school the temptation to buy nice clothes, to look like the other girls in school, outweighed my father's frugality rule—don't buy anything you could do without." True, maybe I could have done without some of the things I liked and wanted, but why should I? I reasoned. After all, this was America and I wanted a piece of the good life it offered. My father's meager weekly allowance for doing all the chores at home, including cooking, was just enough to buy a few personal items and nothing else, especially since he insisted I save half of it for that dreadful "rainy day" lurking nearby.

I was delighted when I presented the summer job idea to my father and he agreed the experience in the working world would be good for me. So, when he sat me down and offered fatherly advice on finding and keeping a job, I was grateful and took his words of wisdom to heart:

"You may not find work right away, so don't get discouraged and don't give up. Keep on searching until you find what you're looking for. And don't be ashamed of honest work or feel that it is beneath you—and always do your best on the job," my father advised. Armed with his blessings and down-to-earth philosophy for success, I ventured out into the world to find work.

In my search for a job I met with some "we have no openings at this time" replies, but that didn't deter me. I kept on knocking on doors until one opened up for me and I was invited in to fill out an application for an immediate opening. I was grateful for a chance to make money, and since I was not afraid of hard work I did not ask about the job description, and was not told. All I knew was that I would be working in an egg factory and how much I would be making—$30.00 per week after taxes, which at the time seemed like a small fortune. I imagined all the great things I could buy for so much money.

"You set three empty buckets and one filled with eggs in front of you," I was instructed once I was hired. "Take one egg at a time from the bucket filled with eggs, break it and sniff it. If the egg smells fresh and looks fresh, you separate the yolk from the white and place the yoke in the yolk bucket and the white in the bucket of whites. If the egg smells bad, (and I was given a very musty one to sniff, which almost knocked me over, so I would know exactly what I had to look for) you throw it in the bucket of bad eggs. The good whites and yolks will then be processed into powder and shipped to army posts all over the country," I was told. "To keep an accurate record of production and to encourage speed, at the end of each day the number of buckets of eggs broken by each worker would be posted on the board, and then totaled at the end of the week," it was pointed out to me. I learned quickly what piecework was all about.

Years have clouded my real reasons for having stayed on that job. Was it for the money alone, or something intangible—a part of whom I was then and still am today? Probably a combination of both. Born under the sign of Taurus the bull—not easily deterred from accomplishing set-forth personal objectives. At any rate, I persevered in the egg factory that summer, breaking and sniffing eggs of all shapes, colors, and odors, even when the eight-hour days seemed like mini lifetimes and I could no longer stomach anything made of eggs.

Prior to my job in the egg factory, eggs in any form were one of my favorite foods. During and following my job in the egg factory, every egg I looked at—broken or whole—reminded me of the bad eggs that I had discarded, and I could no longer eat eggs. It was years before I could make myself eat and enjoy eggs again. But to this day, over a half a century later, I still examine every broken egg carefully before I eat it or serve it to my family or guests. I am happy to report that, over the many years, I have only found a few eggs among the countless good ones, that had to be thrown away because they did not pass my close inspection.

At the end of the first week of work I brought home three crisp ten dollar bills and proudly displayed them on the kitchen table for my father to see when he came home from his night shift. I could hardly wait for the morning and his reaction to my "fortune" and to tell him what I was going to buy for my hard-earned thirty dollars. At breakfast the next day—Saturday—my father smiled and told me he was proud of me because: "Luba, you'll be able to finally put away a nice chunk of money for your future," he said, still smiling as he handed me the bank book he had opened up for me.

"But I thought the money I make is all mine and I get to keep all of it," I protested, perplexed.

"It is all yours, but only half to keep and the other half to save." Then he added, "You save when the times are good so you don't have to worry where the next penny will come from when the times are bad."

Here we go again! It's that "rainy day" that's sure to come one day, according to my father, and I must start preparing for it now whether I want to or not, I thought. I wasn't one bit happy about my father's control over my money, but I knew he meant business when he changed one ten dollar bill to two fives, handed me fifteen dollars and put the other fifteen in the center of the bank book. "I will deposit the fifteen dollars in the bank for you on Monday morning before I go to work, and I'll do that every Monday for the rest of the summer," he told me in no uncertain terms.

I was disappointed that I couldn't keep all the money I earned, but I reluctantly agreed to save half of it. What else could I do? As long as I lived under my father's roof I was obliged to live by his rules—that was only fair—even if I didn't like some of them. And I suppose saving half of my earnings wasn't such a bad idea, after all. At the end of the summer I would still have enough money to buy stylish clothes, shoes…. Things were looking up for me despite having to deal with so many bad eggs.

Walking home from work one evening, I met Nina and a couple of girls I had not seen with her before—they were returning from a shopping spree, Nina said.

"So, what kind of summer job were you able to get with your limited English?" Nina quizzed as the other two girls listened. Without hesitation I told the truth.

"I work in an egg factory and I break and sniff eggs. If the egg is fresh I separate the yolk from the white and put each in separate buckets; if the egg smells bad I throw it in a bucket of bad eggs," I blurted, not caring about the consequences.

Nina and the other two girls doubled up from laughter when they heard what I did on my job. I felt like a laughing stock and in reality I was. I had to say something in my defense to the insensitive trio, especially to Nina, since I thought we were friends.

"I don't expect an apology from your friends, Nina, because I don't know them, but I do expect one from you. You've known me long enough to know I don't appreciate cruel jokes or being made fun of," I told her—and still the three of them continued to laugh. Finally, Nina blurted what was suppose to be an apology, but in my eyes it was another put down:

"Sorry, Luba, but really! How could you stomach the putrid smell of rotten eggs? You could never get me to sniff one of them," she said, still laughing. "I have better things to do with my time," she went on. "Beauty culture school is now my goal and these are my new class-mates," she said and pointed to the other two girls standing next to her, who were still giggling. Needless to say, I was shocked to hear about Nina's latest aspirations!

"What do you mean, 'beauty culture school is now your goal?' What happened to high school and college to become a teacher or maybe even a college professor?" I retaliated, and waited to hear what Nina had to say.

"I changed my course of study and let's leave it at that," Nina answered and whispered something to her new-found friends which caused the three of them to laugh again. At that moment my father's words flashed through my mind like lightning, "Don't be ashamed of honest work," and I decided the time was right to share those words of wisdom with the trio standing in front of me.

"Let me make one thing clear to all three of you," I said. "Breaking and sniffing eggs is not a job I would want to do for the rest of my life or even for another summer, but it is honest work and I'm not ashamed of it. You ought to try it sometime—it would do all three of you a world of good!" I told them, looking straight into each of their eyes. I felt all three of them deserved to hear that, but especial-ly Nina, since I considered her to be my friend and I felt disappoint-ed in her insensitivity, so I went on: "The most important lesson your beauty culture school can teach all of you—that is if you see it through—is compassion and respect for others' feelings. If you never learn that, your beauty will be on the outside only and you'll be empty and ugly on the inside." I spoke my piece and to avoid further con-frontation with Nina and her new friends, I began walking away as fast as I could. Suddenly, the laughter stopped.

"Luba, wait, please!" I heard Nina yell "I want to talk to you!" Nina sounded frantic.

"Why should I wait? I have nothing more to say to you or to your friends," I turned around and yelled back, and continued to walk even faster.

"But I have something to say to you that you should hear. I'm really sorry for being mean to you so many times before, but especially this time." It was the first time I heard Nina sound humble and sincere and I was touched. I slowed down and let her catch up to me while the other two girls remained behind, now silently watching from afar.

"I won't be going back to high school in September, so we won't be seeing each other in school," she said with a sympathetic look in her eyes, not typical of Nina, I knew. "I would like us to continue being friends—I mean real friends—like you told me Pauline and you were, back in your country. From now on, I'll try to be 'compassionate and respectful'—the person you said I should learn to be." She seemed to be speaking from her heart. "Would you like to come to my house to see some great programs on television? And there is a dance coming up.... What do you say, Luba? Can you find it in your heart to forgive me for all my past mistakes? I want us to be friends, please!" Nina pleaded while the other two girls never bothered to move or say anything.

I wanted to believe Nina meant what she said, but I wasn't sure I could trust her. *Did Nina turn a new page in the book of friendship?* I questioned in my mind. Would I be a glutton for punishment if she was merely playing the role to convince me what she wanted me to believe? And when the play was over, would she return to being her old self again?

My father once said, "Give Nina a chance and don't compare her to Pauline," when I complained about her occasional weird behavior. "Nina is her own unique self just as you are," he emphasized. Was I comparing Nina to Pauline and not respecting her for who she was, especially now that her apology seemed so sincere? I silently questioned myself. The fact that Nina apologized and pleaded for forgiveness, while the other two girls remained indifferent, must mean Nina, in her own way, cares. I wouldn't like it if the situation was reversed, and she didn't forgive me for something I did—refused to give me another chance to make things right again.

"Yes, I will come to your house...." And at that magical moment—unbeknownst to either of us at the time—friendship of empathy, respect, and trust between Nina and me took root. One that would grow and bloom through the years, like my petunias on the rooftop. *Almost* as beautiful as the one Pauline and I shared, before merciless fate split us up and put an end to our—one of a kind—friendship! Blessedly, when God closes one door, He never forgets to open another door or a window somewhere else.

Another letter from home arrived and this time it brought the best news we could ever imagine. "There is reason to believe I will be seeing you soon...," my mother wrote. It seemed the immigration laws were getting less stringent and my mother's request to emigrate to America was under serious consideration. Needless to say, this news made my father and me very happy, and we counted the days before we received another letter telling us Mother was on her way. I was glad I had earned enough money in the egg factory to buy her a nice Welcome to America present.

Summer days dwindled down to the last two weeks before the start of fall semester. It was time to say good-bye to endless rows of buckets of eggs waiting to be broken and sniffed. Someone else would have to take my place. I had other plans for the last two weeks of summer vacation, before I went back to school...

Chapter 16

A Vacation in the Country

"What a Difference a Day Makes" is the title of a song dating back to the 1950's. The "twenty-four little hours" alluded to in this enduring classic, are sufficient to make a difference in anyone's life given the right circumstances. They did in mine! One day in the hot summer of 1950, I was breaking and sniffing eggs in a dilapidated egg factory, and the next I was in the world renowned, awe-inspiring, airy Grand Central Station, located in the diversified, spellbound City of New York, waiting for a train which would take me to upstate New York to spend one week in the country, with my aunt, my father's sister.

"I'll see you back here next Saturday!" my father shouted as I boarded the train. Since this was my first time away from home, traveling alone to another unknown destination made me a bit apprehensive, but not for long. As soon as I settled in my window seat, threw the last kiss in my father's direction, and the train left the station, my jitters left too. Excitement and gratitude for the opportunity to be able to see another side of this vast country took over. Vast, beautiful, and diversified, as I learned in my last semester's geography class.

A short time into the trip, brownstone buildings of all shapes began to appear and disappear—no different from the ones in my neighborhood back in the city. As the engine chugged on, so did the disappointing urban landscape—*If that's all there is to the rest of America, then I've already seen it all*, I decided. Discouraged, I rested my head on the headrest and closed my eyes. When I opened my eyes sometime later and looked out, the scenery outside my window literally took my breath away. It was a picturesque countryside the likes of which, I was convinced, could only be found in my Carpathian Mountains homeland and nowhere else on earth, and certainly not in America I knew.

I felt bewildered and emotionally touched to the core by the vistas outside my window: majestic trees reaching up to the sky; meadows dotted with wild flowers; glistening lakes and streams; silhouettes of distant mountain ranges; herds of grazing deer...Occasionally I had to pinch myself and rub my eyes to make sure I was not dreaming.

It was time to humbly acknowledge—less than halfway to my destination—there was much more to this great land than my eyes had seen: the trampled-down concrete sidewalks, factories spewing dark clouds of fumes; weathered-down brownstone dwellings with rusted fire escapes; a littered lot below my father's bedroom window. And even more than the roof garden of boxed petunias from which I drew inspiration to trod on when adversities seemed greater than possibilities.

This eye-opening reality—the abundance of natural beauty in America I was not aware existed—changed forever the way I viewed my adopted country. And it happened at the least expected time and place—traveling to upstate New York to spend a week in the country, visiting with my aunt. Finally, the words to the hymn we sang in school during the weekly assemblies," America The Beautiful," came to life, and I understood why they were immortalized in a song, even though I didn't fully understand all the lyrics.

America is beautiful! I realized. Its unexpected beauty touched the very essence of my being. And to pay tribute to this newly discovered part of America, I was moved to hum the melodies to the hymns whose lyrics I still didn't know verbatim—but vowed to learn—before school opened in September: "America The Beautiful," God Bless America," and "The Star Spangled Banner."

The conductor informed me I would be getting off at the next stop. I gathered my belongings, and although I was glad I would soon be seeing my aunt, I was also saddened because this—one of a kind trip was coming to an end. I moved closer to the door and waited at the exit, hoping to spot my aunt on the platform when I stepped off the train. To my surprise, there were three smiling faces ready to greet me—my Aunt Mary brought along two of her sons, Walter and Bill, my first cousins, a few years older than I. And none of them were strangers to me. I had met them all when they visited my father and me shortly after my arrival in America. The lovely yellow chenille bedspread boasting bold blue flowers which decorated my bed, was the treasured gift they gave me as a Welcome to America present.

"How was your trip?" my aunt asked, once we finished embracing. With great enthusiasm I spoke to all three of them:

"This was an experience of a lifetime! One I will never forget!" I told them.

"Really? That great!" my aunt exclaimed as my cousins looked on, seemingly all three very surprised by my answer. Again, it was my aunt who asked:

"I am curious, and I'm sure we all are, what impressed you most about the trip?"

"The beautiful countryside. It reminded me of home." I answered enthusiastically.

"I see! Would you like to see more of the same?" my aunt offered.

"If it's not too much trouble." I replied politely.

"No trouble!" my aunt smiled as she answered, looking in the direction of her sons. "Boys, there is still plenty of daylight left; how about we take the scenic route back home, so Luba can see more of what she likes—more scenic places." My cousins nodded in agreement and we all walked back to their car, one of them carrying my suitcase.

Soon we were driving through resplendent country roads, the likes of which I had not seen in America: single family homes with white picket fences; fruit trees on hilltops or next to aged barns, so heavy with ripened fruit their branches touched the ground; here and there a single tree-like sunflower, or a field of them, bowing their yellow heads to the smiling sun; sheep, cows and horses grazing in lush grasses. And we arrived at my aunt's home in time to see a sunset no less spectacular than the sunsets I watched long ago and thousands of miles away in the beautiful Carpathian Mountains.

On the following morning, while helping my aunt prepare breakfast, I mistakenly placed a hot frying pan on the kitchen table and burned a frying-pan-size hole in the plastic cover which protected my aunt's lovely hand-embroidered tablecloth. This blunder almost ruined my whole vacation! I had not seen a see-through table-cover before, and thought I had destroyed something very valuable and irreplaceable. I feared I would never be forgiven for my carelessness and decided to hide the hole in the plastic cover from my aunt. To conceal the burned spot, I turned the plastic cover around when my aunt was not looking, and moved the vase of flowers from the middle of the kitchen table to off center, over the round hole. Each time my aunt passed the table, she'd move the vase to its rightful spot—the center of the table. When she wasn't looking, I'd move the vase back over the burned spot. This cat and mouse game went on for a couple of days. Finally, I realized I wasn't winning and I'd better confess, because my aunt was getting annoyed with me. Reluctantly, and with tears in my eyes, I placed the vase where it belonged and pointed to the hole in the plastic cover, not knowing what to expect.

"So that's what this is all about!" my aunt exclaimed and wiped the tears from my eyes. "I'm glad that's all it is and not something serious, like spitefulness or a vision problem," she joshed. "Don't give the plastic cover another thought! I didn't even notice it. Next time I'm in the general store, I'll buy a new one," she assured me and placed a kiss on my forehead.

"So you're not angry with me, and will forgive me for what I've done?" I asked in all seriousness. She giggled as she answered.

"Angry about a piece of plastic? Of course not! There is plenty more plastic where this piece came from. As for forgiveness, there is nothing to forgive. From now on I want to see you smile and enjoy yourself—that's what vacations are for!" Relieved that my worry was now behind me, I was free to enjoy what country living had to offer. And I did—to the fullest.

On the side of my aunt's two-family brick home (another son and his family lived on the top floor), was her pride and joy garden. It was a piece of heaven on earth where flowers of all colors and shapes lived in perfect harmony with each other as well as with their vegetable neighbors and friends; where butterflies frolicked in the sun; fuzzy fat bees and yellowjackets feasted on sweet nectar found in the smiling faces of multicolored flowers. Except for helping my aunt make jams and jellies from the fruit she purchased at outdoor farmers' markets, most of my time was spent in the garden. I basked in the golden sun and dreamed of someday having a house and a garden like my aunt's of my own. After supper each evening, we relaxed on the front porch of the house, and watched the moon and the stars light up the dark country sky. We reminisced about the long-ago life in the humble log home in the Carpathian Mountains, now lost to both of us.

Ironically, we were both born in the same house, most likely on the same bed, fifty-some years apart. And my aunt still remembered a few songs that I knew—some about youth and lost love—which I sang to her. Now and then she would join in, even though her voice was now weak and trembly, her eyes filled with tears. When we finally said good night to the jumping fireflies, the moon, and the stars, the day was complete and peaceful sleep always followed.

A family picnic near the grounds of my aunt's former dairy farm, where all of her five children were raised, was a perfect ending to a perfect vacation. We packed a picnic basket with homemade goodies. To this day, my mouth waters when I remember the taste of the homemade dill pickles and the cheesecake topped with fresh-picked blueberries. I loved the green rolling hills and the clapboard frame house that sat atop a knoll, in clear view of a pepper-and-salt herd of cows that once belonged to my aunt and her family. I rejoiced at the sight of playful calves, some nursing on their patient moms.

Strangely, there was something familiar about the steep-roofed barn on my aunt's former property that baffled me, because it reminded me of home and I didn't know why. And I probably would not have made the connection if my aunt hadn't supplied the missing pieces to the puzzle.

"Your father almost single-handedly built this spacious barn for us when the one that stood on the same site burned down one cold winter night," she lamented as she recalled the unfortunate incident. "Our barn burned down in the height of the Depression. It so happened that your father lost his job and his apartment around the same time. He needed a place to live and we needed a new barn. God works in mysterious ways!" My aunt sighed as she looked in the direction of

139

the now weather-beaten barn, still seemingly very much loved, even though it now belonged to someone else.

So that's why the barn looked so familiar! It was an exact replica of the one on our former property in the Carpathian Mountains, and my father built them both! My mother had told me the story of the monstrous fire that destroyed my aunt's barn in America, and the master builder who raised another one on the site of its ashes. She knew about the fire and the new barn because my father wrote home about it. But this happened before my time, so I never gave it another thought—until now.

Another perfect day came to an end and with it an end to a perfect vacation. In the morning I would board the train for the return trip home to my father in Jersey City, who was waiting for me. Physically, my first vacation in America's countryside had come to an end. Mentally and on some level spiritually, the memories and the benefits I brought back would last a lifetime....

Chapter 17

Hard Work Pays Off

Homeward bound, I was just as impressed by the beauty of the countryside as I was traveling in the opposite direction one week earlier. The picturesque landscape, coupled with the priceless memories I was bringing back home, helped create a bright visionary picture of my future which—at least for the time being—made my spirit soar to heights I dared not even dream about.

Rejuvenated by the fresh air, sunny days, and country-style living, I was excited at the thought of going back to school in a few days to learn all sorts of interesting new things about my new country—its history, geography, the multi-faceted expressions that were typically American, traditions brought here from other parts of the world. And I wanted to travel this road again, and far beyond it, to other parts of this vast and great land. But for now, my place was with my father in our humble three-room, third-floor apartment with a view of the petunia garden on the rooftop. And I was glad to be coming home, because—surprising even to me—I missed my cozy room (my own special place of refuge), to which I could run if I needed a respite from overwhelming problems or even everyday ones, where I could cry when extreme sadness and loneliness invaded my space in the world, or sing and dance when I was happy. And yes! I missed my father, too!

Back at Grand Central Station, my smiling father was waiting for me. From there we had about a half-hour or so travel time on the subway, and about a ten-minute walk from the subway station to our apartment. Safely home, I unpacked my suitcase and proudly displayed several jars of fruit preserves my aunt and I made.

"So that's what made the suitcase so heavy! I thought your vacation included panning for gold in the nearby river, and you found enough to fill an entire suitcase," my father joshed. I learned later in history class what "panning for gold" really meant. On the serious side my father seemed pleasantly surprised and very touched by the gift of love from his sister. And I, too, was delightfully surprised when I discovered a gift-wrapped package with my name on it that my aunt had secretly tucked in between my clothes in the suitcase. I anxiously tore open the package and pulled out a lovely two-piece outfit. "For you, Luba, to wear on the first day of school," the note inside the package read.

I wished I could have thanked my aunt for her generosity right there and then, because I was deeply touched by her thoughtfulness. But since she was hundreds of miles away and we had no telephone to call her, I decided to do the next best thing. When I went shopping for new clothes and supplies for school the next day, I first stopped in a women's apparel store. I bought my aunt a dress with my own money to accompany the thank-you letter I had written. I chose a dress-pattern enhanced by flowers as bright as the ones in her garden. And I was convinced I had sent her a gift so special it could only be found in the store where I bought it. And maybe my aunt thought so too, because she wore that dress every time we visited each other, which was usually once a year in the summer. This gift of appreciation I sent my aunt taught me a valuable lesson: Receiving a gift from the heart and giving one from the heart brings equal pleasure and happiness.

The 1950 summer vacation from school was officially over. The next morning, hopefully following a good night's sleep and a good breakfast, I'd be on my way to school. When night time approached, I set my alarm clock, said my prayers, sank my body into a fluffy featherbed atop my bed, and closed my eyes. A peaceful sleep must have followed because the next thing I knew I was reaching for the turn-off button on my alarm clock. Then I jumped to my feet and walked over to the window to check the weather.

Outside, a light rain was falling and fog hovered over the rooftops. In the distance foghorns blasted warning signals of approaching tugboats and ferryboats on the Hudson River. Yesterday's vibrant petunias on the rooftop were covered by a shroud of misty fog. But today, the first day of school, nothing could dampen my spirit or the enthusiasm carried over from my vacation in the country. Dressed in the outfit my aunt had given me, I felt good about the world around me— ready to face whatever the first day of school and the new semester had in store for me.

Besides a few tense moments on the bus—typical of any new adventure—the first day of the second semester in school passed smoothly and no noteworthy incidents come to mind today. Once I found myself by the statue of Lincoln in the school's vestibule, I felt as if I had never left the place. But I should mention, instead of being relieved Nina was not there to direct me every step of the way, which I resented in the past, I actually missed her watchful eye and jibber-jabber nature. Now if Dana and I wanted to hear any conversation on the bus—to and from school and at lunch time—either she or I had to talk—no more simply relaxing and listening to Nina.

On the way to the last class of the day—typing—I felt a tap on my shoulder. I turned around and was surprised to see John, Nina's neighbor whom I met about a year ago and hadn't run into since. John struggled to communicate with me in his limited Lemko-Rusyn language that he had picked up at home from his mother. He remembered when I couldn't speak English. When he realized I was "almost" as fluent in English as he was, he became embarrassed, shy, and distant. In typing class he sat as far away from me as he could. When the class ended, he deliberately vanished in the crowd so he didn't have to face me, and he followed this pattern throughout the days ahead. In class, however, from time to time, he would glance in my direction and sometimes smile. But when I smiled back, he quickly turned his head in another direction. John was a couple of years ahead of me in high school. His courses were specifically chosen to prepare him for college, so we did not have any of the same classes together, and did not see each other until he elected typing. Even though it was quite obvious John was not interested in developing a friendship with me, I felt an uncanny connection to him, worthy of pursuing. Maybe because his seemingly mild manner reminded me of Peter and he was just as cute as Peter? At any rate, I looked forward to seeing him in typing class each day, and watched for signs that might be interpreted as encouraging, but John remained steadfast in his ways for the rest of the semester and beyond.

"I thought you'd never get back," Nina complained when Dana and I got off the school bus one day. On the way home from her Beauty Culture School, she decided to wait for us, because as she put it, "I miss not having you in my school." Nina jibber-jabbered, as always—all the way home—about her new school and all the wonderful things that were taking place in her life. When we reached the parting corner, she invited me to her house to watch television with her. "Any evening," she emphasized.

A television in one's home in the early fifties was a status symbol, a luxury item most low-income—and even middle-class income—families could not afford. Most people depended on the few friends and family members with tiny-screen television sets for their viewing pleasure, or on the local merchants who purposely left their televisions running in the display windows so that folks without televisions could watch programs from the sidewalks (perhaps hoping the viewers would remember to buy their products as a payback?). On a typical warm summer evening it was not unusual to see crowds of happy people laughing and cheering on the sidewalk in front of a television behind a glass window.

I, on the other hand, was lucky, because I could see my favorite TV shows in the comfort of Nina's family's uncrowded living room. How well I remember Lucy on the `"I Love Lucy" show, crushing grapes in a tub with her feet for the purpose of making wine; Milton Berle—Uncle Miltie—and his "Texaco Star Theater" (His episodes never failed to bring the hardest of laughs, such as Uncle Miltie dressed as a woman clumsily walking in high heels); or Ed Sullivan, hosting the "Toast of the Town" show, featuring different animal acts; or Groucho Marx's "You Bet Your Life" game show; or Arthur Godfrey's "Talent Scout" show.

On the days of the programs I wanted to see, I hurried home from school and immediately got started on my homework. The reward for completing the day's assignments early was an hour or so of television entertainment beyond my wildest dreams. Time has erased the details of most of those early television classics, but the memory of the joy they brought is clear even today, over five decades later. When the show was over, I'd quickly say my thank—yous and good-byes and hurry home to get back to my studies until it was time for bed. Some days it was extra reading. Other days it was learning new words (usually 10—20 each night, depending on the amount of homework) to increase my vocabulary. Occasionally, it was running to cousin Dee's house with problems I couldn't solve myself—less and less as time went on.

Weeks went by and the warm days of summer gave way to a crisp autumn interlude before the arrival of winter. The colorful petunias on the rooftop lost their vibrant blooms. Soon the flowerless and leafless plants would be ravished by Father Frost lurking around the corner. The gingko trees facing my homeroom at school were also letting go of their golden yellow, heart-shaped foliage. The fluttering airborne leaves created a surrealistic scene, conducive to daydreaming, to which I succumbed to one sunny autumn morning.

"Luba, will you please read for us a passage from the Bible this morning?" I faintly heard the teacher ask. Stunned by the unexpected request for which I didn't feel prepared, I gave an abrupt answer.

"No, I can't! I mean, I won't read for you from the Bible this morning!" Apparently my strange, almost belligerent answer amused my classmates. I heard snickers and laughter, and saw the shocked teacher staring at me in disbelief. She then asked that I stay after class because she wanted to talk to me. This unexpected turn of events embarrassed and humiliated me enough to cause a flood of tears which could easily have destroyed my still shaky confidence, if I allowed it to. Fortunately, I quickly realized the folly I had created for myself, and as promptly regained my composure, dried the tears, and silently reasoned with myself. *One regrettable mistake in class is not going to ruin my hard-earned accomplishments to date, or future ones. I will use it to my advantage instead*, I silently vowed. I stayed behind in class, as requested, apologized, and pleaded my case with the homeroom teacher:

"I'm sorry for the way I behaved," I told her, "I'm afraid to read from the Bible, because there are too many words in it I can't pronounce, and I don't want to make a scene in front of my classmates," I confessed. "I meant to talk to you about it, but there never seemed to be the right time," I explained. I then asked if I could take the Bible home following each daily reading, so I could study the passages in the privacy of my own home. I gave her my word she would always find it back on her desk before each morning reading. After some thought she agreed, with a stipulation she could call on me to read a few stanzas from the Bible any time after one month. I assured her I would be ready and happy to oblige.

For the next several weeks, in addition to my regular school work I studied the passages from the Bible, focusing on the few I had least trouble with, and running to Dee's house when I needed help. I also practiced the words and rhythmic movements of warm-up exercises for physical education class, so I'd be prepared to lead the class if called upon at the discretion of the teacher. And I already knew the words to most of the patriotic hymns we sang during the weekly assemblies in school. This progress in areas of shared participation, as well as academics, helped me rise above the status of "that foreign girl," or the less refined expression "the greenhorn," occasionally shot in my direction, which never failed to chip away a piece of my still fragile confidence and spirit. Now I could hold my head high, sing the patriotic hymns, read from the ancient book—The Bible—and conduct warm-up exercises in Physical Education class—all without fear, because I knew I could do it! I was well prepared!

On Saturdays—a day off from school—I cleaned our apartment and washed clothes by hand on a scrubbing board. I hung them on a clothesline outside my father's bedroom window, securing each piece with clothespins. On cold winter days, our frozen clothes looked like grotesque figures from outer space. When the sun went down, I would pull the frozen forms inside the house and place them over the chairs in front of the kerosene stove to defrost and finish drying. This method of washing and drying clothes reminded me, in some ways, of the way we washed and dried clothes back in the Carpathian Mountains, with some exceptions. In winter, we soaked the clothes in

146

a large tub inside the house, scrubbed them on a scrubbing board using homemade soap, and dried them by the wood stove. In summer, we washed clothes in the same manner, but in the nearby river, and instead of a scrubbing board we used a solid chunk of wood—made especially for the purpose of beating out the dirt. The clean clothes were then hung on the wooden fence that enclosed the backyard or a garden area. We had no clotheslines.

The method of washing and drying clothes might not have differed much between the way I was doing it in America and back in my homeland fifty-some years ago, but every other aspect of my life would have differed greatly had I never left my home in the Carpathian Mountains, or the western part of Poland where we were forced to relocate in July of 1947.

In the Carpathian Mountains I probably would have become someone's wife at an early age, whether in love or not—at seventeen or eighteen—and a mother when still in my teens. It was a custom in those days for women to marry early in life—not so for the men. Lucky for them! If someone's daughter or sister was not married by a certain age, twenty-five or so, she would be considered an old maid and a dishonor to her family. Her father would usually offer a larger dowry than for a younger daughter—an extra cow or a piece of land—to make her more desirable to prospective suitors, and wait for someone to ask him for her hand.

Options for young women back then were limited. Besides marriage and family, a farmhand or a maidservant to a more affluent family were the usual routes for young women to take, since education was not readily available for most, at the time. So, if early marriage and family happened to be my destiny, I would have accepted it and made the best of my lot in life, and perhaps even have been happy, since this was the way of life back then and I grew up with that tradition. But in retrospect, I feel blessed that I was spared the "early marriage and family syndrome" of that time and place by immigrating to America when I did. And only because of my parents' foresight. Bless their hearts! My father offered me an opportunity for education and left the marriage and children up to me, and that future "someone" of my choosing, and only if I so desired. And no age stipulation!

I cannot speculate what my life might have been like if I never left western Poland, our home in exile. I did not live there long enough to fully understand the ways of the people, their traditions, and customs. But I must admit I might have had a better chance for education there than back home in the mountains at the time, because education was more readily accessible. Enough speculations about Luba's life that was not to be—back to her life that was meant to be.

To turn the mundane household chores to a less boring task every Saturday, I listened to the Hit Parade on the radio while I worked— the top twenty-one songs popular in the late forties-early fifties. Each week the songs were numerically rated according to their listener appeal. I learned the words and melodies of my favorite ones by singing with the radio in front of a make-believe audience. Some of the songs that touched my heart—not necessarily on the Hit Parade— were: "First Love"; "Autumn Leaves"; "Till I Waltz Again With You"; "I'll Be With You in Apple Blossom Time"; "Look for the Silver Lining"; "Hello, Young Lovers"; "Mockingbird Hill"; "Unforgettable"; "Green, Green Grass of Home"; and a ditty titled "How Much Is That Doggie in the Window."

My favorite radio serial program was: "Stella Dallas—the Backstage Wife." I would hurry home from school every day to hear the next half hour of Stella's travails in life, who if I remember correctly, happened to be an abused housewife. I still remember, many decades later, the excitement I felt for Stella when she asserted herself in belittling situations. I actually cheered even though no one heard me, and certainly not Stella. Was I unknowingly cheering for women's rights or simply human rights? I think so!

The movie that impressed me most in the early fifties in terms of actors was "The Ten Commandments," starring Charlton Heston. But it wasn't Mr. Heston, who so brilliantly portrayed Moses, that I fell madly in love with while watching this classic. It was a co-star named John Derek, who played the role of Joshua. My love affair with Joshua (John Derek) lasted throughout my high school years. While other girls in school decorated their locker doors with pictures of many movie stars, my door had only one. It was an autographed picture of John Derek given to me by Nina in the spirit of friendship.

And I treasured that gift for years to come. To this day, many decades later, it remains an important part of my memorabilia. It is a reminder of the teenage stage in life I almost missed, but I am glad I caught at least the tail end of it. As time passed and I went to the movies more often, I became enamored with other movie stars, male and female, some of whom became my role models. Among them were: Doris Day, Betty Grable, Debbie Reynolds, Grace Kelly, John Wayne, Bing Crosby, Gary Cooper, and Perry Como. But, like first love, John Derek was my first movie idol and for years no one else could take his place in my heart.

Before the end of the second semester (end of 1950, beginning of 1951), I successfully read to the class the Twenty-third Psalm from the Bible. This psalm became my favorite passage in the Bible and to this day I call upon it in time of need. I was randomly picked and successfully led the class in warm-up exercises in Physical Education class, too. There was nothing left to be afraid of. There was only a steady pace of work which I knew I could handle. I could almost see the top of the fourth hill and the star that shone upon it—which happened to resemble me, of all people!

One warm evening as I sat in front of the window in our apartment, absorbed in my studies, I saw the lady on the rooftop across from me puttering in last year's flower boxes. I realized it was spring again, and she was planting her petunias once again, much to my pleasure. The end of the third semester in school and summer vacation were fast approaching—half of the sophomore year was over.

My report card showed I passed all the subjects with flying colors. Ironically, what I feared most at the beginning of high school—shorthand—became my favorite subject, next to geography and history, two subjects that helped me understand and appreciate the sacrifices of our predecessors on behalf of our great nation. As for stenography, once I grasped the concept of Pitman Shorthand—later replaced by other, simpler methods of shorthand writing—I felt in control of a secret language all my own. Because I enjoyed the challenge of stenography, and was good at it, I used it in any way I could: I kept a diary in shorthand; took notes in class; took dictation from the radio; and copied passages from magazines and newspapers.

When school closed for the summer, of 1951, it was time to find a summer job again. For the record, I stayed away from the egg factory. I saw a sign in a Five and Ten Cent Store window, "Hiring," and tried my luck. I filled out a simple application, handed it to the manager and was on my way out when I heard my name called.

"Luba! Wait!" the lady yelled. "I want to talk to you."

The next day I was standing behind a notions counter in a Five and Ten Cent Store, selling ribbons, threads, and yarn. About a month later I was given a promotion and a nickel more per hour. On the new job I collected and counted money from about fifteen cash registers, balanced each day's receipts against the register tapes, and deposited the proceeds in the store's account in the bank.

I was thrilled with my promotion, my raise, and with what the manager had said to me. "We observed you and liked what we saw— a hard-working, trustworthy young lady, and that's why we promoted you so quickly and gave you a raise." My new job presented a challenge that tested my knowledge of math, accuracy, and dependability, and I loved the responsibility. Also, my pay of $35 a week was considered good money in the early fifties. I was doing well on my summer job and I was happy.

One day the manager overheard me talking about going back to school at the end of summer vacation, and that's when everything changed for me. She was under the impression that I was not going back—hence the promotion and the raise. This misunderstanding created a problem between us. She tried to convince me that to quit my job would be a huge mistake. Rather, she suggested, I should quit school. During the next few days she put pressure on me to quit school. Her power of persuasion put me in a state of confusion. On one hand I liked the job and the money it paid. On the other hand, I desperately wanted to graduate from high school, and hopefully continue with further education. In my dilemma I turned to my father for advice.

"Do what you feel is right for you," was his hesitant answer. But I didn't know what was right for me at that point. Both options seemed reasonable. One day I was quitting school and staying on the job, and the next day I was resigning from the job and going back to school. I was tired of this yo-yo feeling and I was frightened. What if I made a wrong decision? Then suddenly out of nowhere the right answer came. It was as if the "gentle voice"—one who helped me choose the right path in the past—was speaking to me. Again!

"Your father wants you to stay in school but he wants that decision to come from you! Say No! to the job and Yes! to school. You will make your father—and yourself—very happy in the end." That did it! Of course I wanted to be happy in life, and I wanted the same for my father! "I'm going back to school!" I shouted at the top of my voice.

"I trusted you to make the right decision and you did. I'm proud of you, Luba!" my father said with a smile when he heard my resolute answer. He then opened his wallet and pulled out a crisp ten dollar bill—a small fortune in those days, especially for someone like my father, who hung on to the Great Depression mentality for dear life. "For you from me, Luba! Go buy something nice for yourself for school."

Chapter 18

My First Date

Not all flowers bloom simply because Mother Nature declares it is spring! Many bloom in the summer and others in the fall. And all are lovely in their own way and time! "To everything there is a season...." By the same token, I did not experience the joy of the "real" date until I was almost nineteen years old. Chronologically speaking, I began dating in the late autumn of my teenage stage of life. This is not to say the crushes and heartbreaks of that hormone-packed period bypassed me. Not at all! I've had crushes and heartbreaks like everybody else. And I know I've caused a few heartbreaks in return. That's how love works—"puppy love" in my case—because I wasn't ready for "real" love until other priorities in my life were first taken care of.

One cold late afternoon in February of 1952—midway in pursuit of my high school diploma—my homework time was interrupted by an unexpected knock on the door. I rushed to see who was on the other side. It was Nina. She looked as if her world had either collapsed or was on the verge of collapsing, unless I came to her rescue:

"Please stop what you're doing and come for a walk with me. I need to talk to you about something very important," she blurted, her eyes searching for understanding.

I was nowhere near finished with my assignment and wanted to say, No! I can't do it, because I have too much homework." But Nina seemed desperate, so I agreed to take a break from my studies and venture into the cold for the sake of our friendship. Still I questioned what could be so urgent that Nina couldn't discuss it in our cozy, warm apartment, and while I worked on my homework? On the way down she explained.

"I need your full attention and I know I can't have it unless you're away from your books," she told me. Once outside, trudging on the lightly snow-covered sidewalk in the dusk, Nina opened up:

"I met someone very nice in school. He asked me out, but my mom wouldn't let me go with him unless we double-date with another couple. I was wondering if you'd do me a big favor?" she asked in a quivering voice.

"What kind of favor?" I asked, bewildered. Nina came right to the point.

"Would you go out with John, so we can be a foursome? I already asked him and he said it would be okay with him, if it's okay with you," she assured me.

"You asked John before you checked with me? I can hardly believe your nerve!" I reprimanded her.

"Sorry, Luba, please forgive me and say yes," she begged.

"Maybe I can forgive you this one time, and if I do, you must promise this will not happen again," I warned her.

"I promise," Nina crossed her hands over her heart. But I wasn't finished yet.

"If you had checked with me first, I could have told you John never spoke to me when we were in typing class together. And now, he walks in the opposite direction if he happens to see me in school while changing classes. I think he hates me! So why would I want to go out with him or he with me?" I angrily stated my case.

"Leave everything to me and don't worry about anything, just say yes, please!" she pleaded.

To desperate Nina, the tiny smirk on my face and a pause while considering her unusual request meant a "Yes" answer.

"Thanks a million! We'll meet at your house on Saturday at seven," I heard her say loud and clear, as she quickly disappeared into the dusk without giving me a chance to make up my mind.

The date was set for Saturday at seven—only two days away and without a firm "Yes" answer from me. I felt I was being taken advantage of, but I also felt that maybe I should help Nina—this one time—

and let the chips fall where they may, hopefully in my direction. My father gave an approving smile when I asked if he had any objections to my going out on a date with John, Nina, and her friend.

The next two days were filled with apprehension as well as anticipation, also some fear that I would meet John between classes (John was now a senior), and not know what to say to him—that is, if he didn't speak to me first. I wished I knew an easy way to melt the icy wall between us, but I didn't. And I had no idea why John agreed to double-date with me. I finally decided perhaps we were both trapped by Nina's overpowering nature, and left it at that.

When Saturday came and the inevitable moment drew closer, my heart decided to play a few tricks on me. It began beating fast and furiously, the like of which I had not experienced before, which scared me half to death. *I should try to get out of this trap*, a thought came to mind. Maybe I should pretend I am not at home and ignore the knock on the door when the trio arrives. Or tell the truth: "Suddenly I feel ill." My mind was racing as fast as my heart, searching for a last-minute solution to my dilemma, until it was interrupted by what happened next:

"Luba, you're acting like a coward. Calm yourself down and greet your friends with a cheerful smile when they arrive. There is nothing wrong with you—once you calm down, your heart and mind will calm down, too. Now, take a deep breath and relax—think of the fun you're about to have." The message was loud and clear even though no actual words were spoken, and—as usual—I was alone in the house.

At the third rap on the door, I put on a smile and slowly unlocked the door. I couldn't ignore the advice of the "gentle voice" in my head. It had never steered me wrong before.

The first thing Nina did when I invited the three of them in was thrust out her right hand to show off the corsage of pink baby roses on her wrist. While I was admiring Nina's flowers, John spoke.

"I'm glad you like the rose corsage, Luba," and handed me one just like it with a smile, which threw me into a state of confusion again. I had not seen a rose corsage before, much less received one. And from John of all people! Dumb founded, I stood in awe, holding the corsage in my shaking hands, unable to speak. I felt as if something had become stuck in my throat and no sound could penetrate through. Again, the "gentle voice" in my head saved the moment:

"Luba! Slip the corsage on your wrist and say thank you. Tell John you appreciate his thoughtfulness, and don't forget to smile." I did as instructed. Slipped the corsage on my right wrist, put my coat on with John's gentlemanly help, locked the door behind me, and the four of us were on our way. Where to, I didn't know.

The newly fallen layer of snow was now frozen, which made a clear, crisp sound under our feet as the four of us walked. Nina and her friend held hands and even exchanged a few kisses on the way. John and I kept our hands to ourselves, and there was mostly silence between us. But, surprisingly, I was beginning to feel at ease in John's company anyway.

I had heard of "The New Victory Hall" before—only a few blocks from my home—and the wonderful dances that were held there every Saturday featuring live, well-known bands, but I had never had the pleasure of being at one of those dances. So it was no wonder my disappointment in Nina's "thoughtlessness" suddenly gave way to appreciation for her "thoughtfulness," when we reached our destination, "The New Victory Hall." A new world to me in every sense of the word.

I wasn't much of a dancer in those days, but I managed to hop to the fast Polka beat without stepping on John's toes or tripping over my own feet, or his. There was practically no conversation between us the entire evening until the last dance, which came around much too soon for my liking. When the clock struck twelve and the band played "Good Night Ladies," John began to talk about his plans for the future.

"After graduation from high school in June, I'll be going to college. When I get my art degree from Pratt, it will be my turn to give two years of my life to Uncle Sam," he divulged.

"You'll be going into the army?" I asked, since I didn't know what else to say.

"Yes, unfortunately—or fortunately, depending on how one chooses to look at it. The way I look at it, as long as I owe some time to Uncle Sam (the draft was in effect), I might as well make the best of it and learn from the experience, too," he said with a nervous smile.

155

And that was about the extent of our conversation that night. But it was enough to leave a lasting impression in my mind. And though our young lives took different paths in the interim, the memory of that special first date with John, the corsage of pink baby roses, John's gentle manner and sweet smile, lingered on. Our friendship was destined to rekindle several years later when our paths crossed again. When we were two mature adults with an abundance of everyday experiences derived from life and different kinds of relationships over the years, most of which—for one reason or another—culminated in broken hearts, fortunately capable of self-healing in time. When we knew what we wanted out of life and were comfortable enough within ourselves to share each other's thoughts and dreams....

Chapter 19

Reunited at Last

Spring 1952 found me successfully completing the fifth semester—the first half of my high school junior year—looking forward to another challenging summer job, which would, hopefully, encompass my newly-acquired skills thus far: shorthand, typing, and bookkeeping. So when the telegram from my mother reached us in the late Spring "Arriving in New York on the Polish Ocean Liner *Batory*," my already high spirit took off like an eagle—upwards through the limitless sky, eventually landing on "Cloud Nine!" My spirit's residence in that "special" place in the clouds was short-lived, however. Soon, reality appeared and knocked it back to earth where it belonged!

Living in different parts of the world all those many years, my parents would need time and space to renew what was left of their relationship, shattered by circumstances. This fact hit me like a ton of bricks one night, only days before my mother's arrival. What would my life be like living with them under the same roof, sharing a small kitchen and two tiny side-by-side bedrooms…? Such thoughts and worries were now consuming most of my time. I was wasting precious time and energy, I realized, when another reality slapped me in the face only two or three days before my mother's arrival:

"Luba, once again you're jumping ahead of yourself! Your worries about the future will not change the future. But hard work and good deeds will have a shot at it. So get to work!" Again, that inner "gentle voice" saved me from myself at that precarious moment—and maybe even opened the door to a brighter future for the three of us!

There was work to be done before we welcomed my mother into our humble home. Suddenly, I wanted to be the one to see that everything was done right! I cleaned the house from top to bottom. And to give the home a bright and cheerful look, I convinced my father to buy new curtains for all the windows, as well as area rugs for the floors in all three rooms. We also purchased a large scenic picture to replace the small one hanging next to the clock above the kitchen table, already enhanced by a flower-shade lamp, my father received as a reward for purchasing most of our food-items in the same grocery store. We were now ready to bring my mother—and my father's wife—home!

On the day of my mother's scheduled arrival I was excused from school. Even school had to take a back seat in honor of this extraordinary event. The morning of the arrival I woke up earlier than usual and prepared a special dinner for us, when we returned home with my mother. My father hired a driver with a car, and we were on our way, bouquet of spring flowers in hand to get her.

The years have obliterated the reason why we didn't get to the seaport on time. Was it our fault, or did the ship arrive ahead of schedule? At any rate, when we found my mother she was in a state of desperation. "Something horrible must have happened to my family on the way here. What will I do now?" I heard her lament, before she realized we were standing beside her. She looked so pathetic in her peasant dress and tasseled woolen kerchief wrapped around her head, even though the day was sunny and quite warm. Still in her forties, she looked more like a woman in her late seventies or older. The years since I left home had treated her so unkindly that I hardly recognized my mother, and my father would have passed her up if I hadn't been there to stop him.

Finally together, we kissed away the tears from her distraught eyes and face, and assured her all would be well now that we were together. We packed her meager belongings in the trunk of the car and headed for home across the Hudson River, via the Holland Tunnel, to Jersey City. On the way home, as well as at home, my mother hardly spoke. She showed no emotions about her new surroundings—good or bad—nor did she compliment my dinner, which she barely touched. A day or so later she revealed the reason for her strange behavior. "The arduous ocean voyage almost killed me. I had been sick from the moment I boarded the ship until we docked in the New York Harbor, many days later. I gave up hope of ever seeing you again," she shed tears as she told us.

I understood the reasons why my mother acted the way she did for the first few days. But when her indifference toward me remained after several weeks—and not towards my father—I began to feel resentful. She and he appeared very happy, and talked a lot, but only to each other. Being the youngest in the family, my two older brothers never seemed to mind when, as a child and even beyond childhood, I clung to my mother like glue to paper, because I would leave them free to do their own "boy" things. So, growing up, I had no competition vying for my mother's love and attention—until now.

I felt mature enough to understand my mother had a husband now, and my father a wife. A husband and wife who hadn't seen each other in well over a decade, and needed time and space to recapture and rekindle the love that had been stifled by time and distance. But I didn't understand why they deliberately seemed to be leaving me out of our little family circle. *Don't they know I need them, too?* I questioned resentfully.

I felt completely left out of their tight relationship. The loving mother I knew turned out to be the stranger who took away my new-found father. And the father who I thought loved me unconditionally chose to love only one person—his wife. Together they reflected on life before my existence, and planned a future that did not include me. My parents seemed perfectly happy to spend every minute just with each other. It was obvious they didn't need me, which made me very sad. In spite of everything, I was still vying for their attention and love, seemingly to no avail.

A few days into the summer vacation I went hunting for a job. And I found one that would challenge my skills in shorthand, typing, and bookkeeping, as I hoped. Surely my parents would be impressed, and would have questions. A discussion would follow and I would have my parents back, I dared to think. But that didn't happen. When I told them about my great job, they listened but only halfheartedly, and asked no questions, as I had hoped, afterwards. Instead, they chose to go back to rehashing the events of times and places I knew nothing about, and I celebrated the moment of triumph alone, or so it seemed.

One day I heard them talking about moving to a larger apartment, but my input was not sought. That's when I began to entertain thoughts of moving out as soon as I graduated from high school in a year. I reasoned my parents would not miss me, and maybe they'd even be better off without me. And I didn't need selfish parents, either, I concurred with myself.

The family-operated electrical fixture business where I worked during that long-ago summer vacation in 1952 was a homey, second floor office space with a business on the ground floor—about fifteen minutes by bus from my home. The owner, his wife, their daughter, and I were the four people who saw to it that business ran smoothly on all levels. The office itself looked more like a private apartment than a business. There were flowerpots with blooming plants on every windowsill, and some hanging from the ceiling. The owner took care of the business and his wife kept the books and ordered the merchandise. Their daughter tended the switchboard and did some general office work. I was the all-around helper. I took light dictation, typed letters on the manual Underwood typewriter, helped with simple bookkeeping, and relieved the switchboard operator (their daughter) when she took her lunch breaks or on her days off.

At first the work seemed somewhat intimidating, but not for long. Almost from the very beginning, the members of this family-run business took me into their fold. Everything I did for them was well appreciated, and so was I. I felt comfortable in their midst and with the money they paid me—$40 per week. On hot and humid days, many times, I wished I didn't have to leave the comfortable air-conditioned office to go home at the end of the day to face my parents, who continued to have eyes only for each other. My place of work became my home away from home, in all respects. It was another temptation to quit school and move out of my parents' house that much sooner. Just as I considered the big decision, and was ready to spring the news on my parents, they surprised me with news of their own.

"Luba, how would you like to go on a vacation with me before you go back to school?" my mother asked.

"A vacation? Where to? And why would you want to take me, and leave Father at home? " I questioned her.

"To Seymour, Connecticut," my mother answered and went on. "I received a letter from your Uncle Sam, my brother, and he invited all of us to spend some time with him and his family. Your father can't take time off from work to go with me. I was wondering if you could leave your job a little sooner than you planned, so you and I could go together. You'll be leaving it soon anyway, to go back to school." She waited for my response, but when I didn't answer, she continued. "Uncle Sam left for America shortly after I was born, so I didn't get to know him. But I would surely love to meet him now. And I have another brother in Seymour, "Uncle Victor, who emigrated to America before I was born. So you see, there is a double reason to visit Connecticut."

"No, there is a triple reason," my father chimed in "You, Luba, need a vacation. You've been working and studying very hard, and have accomplished so much. You deserve some time off for fun, before another year of learning begins for you. And it would be nice for you to get to know the rest of your family in America, and spend some time with your mother, alone. What do you say, Luba?" Was I hearing things right? I thought to myself. The words—studying hard, need to spend time with Mother alone, get to know the rest of the family in America, weren't making much sense. My parents didn't worry about my needs, only theirs! Their seemingly genuine concern for me at the moment only confused me. Were they for real?

"I need time to think this over," I finally told them. After a day or so, weighing all the pros and cons, I made a decision and gave them my answer.

"Yes, I'll take the vacation," I told my parents. Which factor tipped the scale in favor of vacation and school, I wasn't quite sure. A chance to spend time with my mother, my parents' turn-around attitude in my favor, or the spot on the wall in my room, awaiting my high school diploma? Probably all three!

I left my job in the middle of August, with a little over two weeks of vacation time, before the start of the fall semester. The family I worked for appeared saddened when I gave them my notice to leave.

They offered me a full-time job, with an increase in salary. When I turned their offer down in favor of school and the possible renewal of my relationship with my mom, the owner's wife asked me to check back with her the next summer vacation or after I graduated from high school. If they still needed help, I would be rehired with a substantial increase in salary. A great offer! When the moment to say good-bye arrived, we all hugged each other and shed a few tears. I knew I was giving up a family—not my own, but one who treated me as one of their own. A priceless gift—one to be treasured!

Happy tears flowed like streams in springtime when my mother and her brothers saw each other for the first time. We kids, their children, looked on in disbelief, wondering when they would stop embracing. When they finally did, Uncle Sam recalled an incident that happened almost a half century earlier which had never stopped haunting him. Facing my mother, he sobbed.

"You were only several weeks old when our father died. His body was laid out in our house. Psalms from the Holy Book were read and prayers recited for two straight days and nights. Our mother was beside herself, as this was the second husband she'd lost. The night before the burial, she asked me—and I obeyed—to roll you over our father's dead body in hopes that by so doing, our father would soon call you to live with him in heaven." I had not heard of or experienced a grief of that magnitude in all of my fourteen years living there, so I was just as shocked as my cousins to hear that astounding account.

"We were very poor," my uncle continued, "and our mother was convinced you'd be better off with our father in paradise than with her on earth, unable to feed another mouth. There were seven of us to feed already, not counting you." When Uncle Sam had finally freed his heart and soul of the secret he had carried with him all these years, he bowed his head and fervently acknowledged, "God knew better than to listen to me, and today I thank Him for His Divine Wisdom. Praise His Holy Name Forever!" he whispered and hugged his sister again.

We were welcomed into my uncles' homes with bouquets of flowers, and treated royally for the entire time we spent with them— almost two weeks. We would have lunch in one uncle's house and dinner in the other uncle's house (Mother and I always pitched in) and vice versa, day after day. But for my mother and me, their gardens were where the renewal of our mother/daughter relationship took place. Every morning and evening we walked the paths in my uncles' gardens of flowers and vegetables, catching up on years of separation and planning for the better ones ahead. There was so much to talk about! And we both found the surroundings conducive to reminiscing, and for patching up the splits in our mother/daughter relationship.

Once we rehashed things that were important to us, my mother confessed. "This vacation was especially planned for the two of us. Your father could have arranged to take time off from work, but he chose not to. We both realized, and agreed, you and I needed some time alone, because we had grown apart. In an effort to renew our own relationship, your father and I neglected you," my mother admitted with head bowed low. "That will no longer go on," she assured me, as she placed a kiss on my forehead.

My plans for leaving home any time soon became dust in the wind as my mother and I walked and talked in her brothers'—and my uncles'—gardens.

Chapter 20

Graduation

The time my mother and I spent in the Connecticut countryside was less than two weeks, but the benefits we brought back proved timeless and priceless for all three of us. For reasons not completely understood at the time—and to this day—our lives together changed for the better, starting with day one of our return from that memorable vacation.

"Spending all this time without both of you seemed like an eternity. I didn't only count the days, I counted the hours until your return. How on earth did I ever survive all those many years not knowing if my wife and children were even alive? From now on, don't even think about leaving me behind, should you decide to take another vacation!" he joshed as he embraced and kissed us both at the same time, again and again. There was no doubt in my mind my father loved and missed us both. I felt elated and for a good reason. I had my parents back!

The days of the summer vacation dwindled down to the last two. It was time once again to go shopping for school supplies as well as for some new clothes. Yes, beautiful and stylish clothes—like other girls in school wore—likes of which I couldn't buy until I began earning my own money, half of which I felt obliged to give to my father to deposit into my savings account for that inescapable "rainy day" he always preached about. I was closing the door behind me on the way to hit the stores when I heard my mother call:

"Luba, wait! I want to go with you." Surprised but delighted, I came back and waited for her.

I knew my mother had received monetary gifts from her brothers in Connecticut, but the way she wanted to spend her gift money came as another surprise.

"Luba, I want to buy you some new clothes for school, the kind fancy American girls wear," she told me. And she opened her wallet to show me how much money she actually had, still unable on her own to determine the dollars' true worth. I tried to dissuade her from spending her "love" money on me. I suggested she buy a special memento for herself with it, instead. But she wouldn't hear of it:

"The best memento for me will be a gift for you," my mother insisted. "Seeing you in something nice that I bought with my own money will make me very happy—so please let me."

"Only if I can buy you something too," I answered. She smiled and nodded in agreement. Neither of us had enough money to buy what we really wanted for each other, but that didn't matter. What mattered was that we three individual entities—Mother, Father, and I, their daughter—-were now one family who cared about and respected each other.

I can still visualize the smile and glow on my mother's face when she first put on this impressive-looking—regretfully inexpensive—aqua and white graduated bead necklace I bought for her—"a token of our renewed relationship as mother and daughter," I told her. She wore that humble string of beads day in and day out for as long as she lived (she died at age 61), whether it matched her outfit or not. I found it among her possessions after her death. This simple but price-less piece of jewelry given to my mother during her lifetime holds a special place in my heart to this day, over four decades later. It repre-sents to me love strong enough to defy the divide between here and the great beyond.

My gift from my mother was a long black velvet skirt and a green short-sleeve sweater with a touch of black to match the skirt. I wore this lovely set on the first day of school that long ago September of 1952 and on special occasions for several years thereafter. How I final-ly disposed of it is now obliterated by time, but the memory of it is still intact. Following that first shopping spree with my mother, she and I enjoyed similar outings almost every Saturday. Prior to shopping for food and/or clothes, we never failed to stop in a luncheonette for a grilled cheese sandwich and a drink. And while we enjoyed our special treat we talked about things that were important to us, like in the past. Some Saturdays only I talked and she listened. And although she didn't always understand everything or the depth of my concerns, because she came from a different culture, it was still great to have a mother who never tired of listening to me—one human being who would not betray or judge me unfairly, loved me unconditionally, and gave counsel only when I asked for it, or in her opinion, I needed it.

Time passed and with it came the end to my junior year. In January 1953 I joined the group of the high school elite—the seniors. The following summer I was rehired by my favorite people in the electrical business.

The expression, "time flies when you're having fun," applies perfectly to the way I spent my last semester in school. At the beginning of high school, struggles and fears of real or imagined inadequacies dominated my life, so I wished for time to pass quickly; instead it dragged on. When I gained control of my life through hard work and perseverance, and wanted to savor the feeling of success, I wished for time to slow down; instead the days and weeks rushed by like water after a heavy rain storm, into oblivion. The precious few weeks before graduation were busy but rewarding ones, and I wished there were more of them.

Our class rings arrived! I placed mine on my left index finger and vowed not to take it off, ever! This treasured memento represented to me the victory over all my adversities of the past and the accomplishments which changed me to a new "Me"—ready to enter the business world with confidence, because my skills matched the requirements of the companies seeking help: able to type eighty words a minute on a manual typewriter; able to take dictation at one hundred and twenty words a minute; proficient in bookkeeping... .

In addition to my physical skills, my outward personality and attitude must have made a positive impression on the recruiter from a well-known-at-the-time, prestigious company—Western Electric—now bearing other names (the reputable Baby Bells). I was hired on the spot before I even graduated from high school, and for an excellent well-paid secretarial position which I enjoyed for many years. Eventually I worked myself up to an executive secretary's position with Boyle-Midway (no longer in existence), which at the time was a division of another prominent conglomerate—American Home Products, from which, after years of service, I retired. For the record, American Home Products Corporation is now boasting a new name—Wyeth. Between my secretarial positions, I savored several rewarding years working with school children as a teacher's aide for the Cranford Board of Education in the beautiful township of Cranford, New Jersey "my home sweet home," for over 40 years. The difference my well-earned high school diploma made in my life surpassed even my imagination.

Life was good for all three of us! The Christmas prior to my graduation we actually bought and decorated a Christmas tree in our newly acquired, much larger apartment, a couple of blocks away from our first apartment, and also on the third floor. Our first Christmas tree was not a real one—like I remembered my brothers used to bring home from our own forest long ago—but to me it looked every bit as real.

We placed it in front of the floor-to-ceiling, lace-adorned double window in the living room, hung a string of colored lights on its branches and topped it with a star. But instead of the traditional glass ornaments, my mother and I baked colorful sugar cookies and hung them on the tree. We also decorated the tree with green and red apples and candy wrapped in glittering pieces of paper. I made a long paper chain and paper snowflakes and hung them on the tree, too— all in remembrance of the past Christmas traditions back home. Our tree looked beautiful and we could pull off the goodies and enjoy them while we reminisced of Christmases long ago in the Carpathian Mountains and made wishes for future ones in America. There were never any gifts under our Christmas trees back in the log home in the old country, so we followed that tradition too. However, the American tradition of celebrating Christmas with gifts galore under the Christmas trees took over soon enough.

Ironically, the two floor-to-ceiling windows in the kitchen of our new apartment led to a flat roof suitable for clothes lines and enough space for several boxes of petunias, which I planted the very first spring in our new home and thereafter. Now we had a spacious apartment with three bedrooms, an enormous kitchen, and a sizable living room, enhanced by all-new furniture. In addition, I gained a place for my own petunia garden on the rooftop from which to draw inspiration. What else could I possibly want? Or as I hear young people's expressions today, "how cool is that!"

The first time we celebrated in our new apartment with a houseful of guests was when I graduated from high school in January 1954. After the tearjerker ceremony in school, we returned home to celebrate with friends and relatives. Among the people who came to rejoice with me on my special day was John. He came with Nina, his neighbor, but my parents invited him. My mother told me later, "Nina told us John was on a winter break from college and we thought his presence would make your happy day even happier." They were right! But how did they know? Other guests at my graduation party included my aunt (my mother's sister Mary) and two of her children, Cousin Dee (of course), and two of her brothers, and a sister as well as her parents.

We feasted on my mother's stuffed cabbage, perogies (ravioli-like dumplings), home-made breads, cakes, and wine. I displayed my yearbook, named "The Quill," and pointed to the "Who's Who" page. My picture was there. I was chosen—along with a male classmate—As "Most Respected" in the class of eighty-some students. This was an honor bestowed on me I never expected.

My parents beamed with pride as they showed off my report card. "Can you beat this—my Luba worked herself up to an honor student," my father boasted shamelessly as my mother looked on with an ear-to-ear smile. But my father failed to see a couple of "B's" among the "A's," which placed me a notch below the honor roll. In my parents' eyes I was an honor student, just the same. This was the happiest and proudest moment of my life thus far. I had reached the goal I set for myself. I had climbed all four hills to the very top and now it was time to enjoy the view as promised by the "gentle voice" of the past.

I felt richly blessed that my parents were there to share in my happiness! But, oh! how I wished my brothers could have been there, too. "Be patient, Luba," the gentle voice in my head chimed in once again. "This is one case in which everything that could have been done to expedite the desire of your heart has been done! You need only to wait and trust. Can you do that?" *Yes! and thank you, "gentle voice," I will wait and trust, because I trust you*, I whispered.

My graduation present from my parents was a lovely crystal necklace with matching earrings. I still have the set and I wear it on special occasions. Two gold and diamond watches—one for me and the other for my mother with a note—"To my special pride and joy ladies," were post-graduation and Welcome to America gifts from my father, even though he himself never owned one. I framed my diploma in a silver frame, hand-crafted by my talented and proud father, and I hung it above the bed in my room in the space reserved for it. Following my high school graduation, I immediately enrolled in a local college where I attended evening classes after work. *High school will not, be the end of my formal education—not if I can help it*, I vowed!

Chapter 21

Rainy Days!

Our happy family life in the new apartment was short-lived—a brief period of three to four years of calm before the raging storm. Without warning our lives took a downhill slide, landing on what appeared to be an endless bumpy road. It all began one day in the latter part of 1956—the exact date(s), also true in a few other instances throughout this autobiography, now stifled by many layers of years.

After a busy, somewhat trying day at work, I looked forward to a relaxing dinner at home with my parents. But instead of finding my mother in the kitchen putting the final touches to our evening meal, like on most evenings, I found a note on the table which would forever change the way we lived.

"We're at ——- Hospital. Come as soon as you can!" the note read. I knew I was in for some bad news, but I was not prepared for what I found when I located my father in the critically-ill patients' area, seemingly unconscious, while my pathetic-looking mother hovered over him helplessly. In spite of the grim situation in front of her, my mother still embraced me as she pointed to my comatose father, directing my attention to his left leg submerged in a cradle of ice.

"What happened?" I asked my tearful mother. She told me what she knew.

"I rushed your father to the doctor because the pain in his left knee he's been complaining about lately got so bad he almost passed out on me several times, after you left for work. The doctor at the office examined his leg, and told us to go straight to the emergency

170

room at the hospital. In the emergency room, other doctors inspected the leg, took some pictures, and then whisked him away to an operating room. He was brought back unconscious and the operated-on leg buried in ice, which to me spells bad news, but so far no one came to the room to explain to me what went wrong. That's all I can tell you," my mother blurted, then blew her nose, dried her teary eyes and lowered her visibly exhausted body to a chair next to my father's bed. I needed to speak to someone in charge and quickly. I wanted to know what went wrong during the operation to cause this ghastly situation. And what was being done for my father now! At that moment, a saintly-looking nun stepped into the room and walked directly toward me.

"Are you the patient's daughter?" she inquired. I nodded and waited for her to speak. "I need to talk to you privately; please follow me," she requested. She seemed aware of my mother's inability to understand the English language, because she did not ask her to come along. The sister introduced herself to me in a strange way:

"I am Sister ——- Head of the surgical department here, but don't let on you know me or my name—you'll see why, after I tell you what you and your mother must know and do. Pay attention so you'll understand what we're dealing with here; ask questions only if you need to." So far I had no questions, but I knew she was not finished.

"Your father underwent an emergency surgery for a huge, non-malignant tumor behind the knee of his left leg. The tumor's roots were intertwined around numerous other veins, dangerously cutting off the blood supply to other crucial body parts," she rattled off. I asked her to speak slower, only to be told, "there is no time to dawdle," and she continued on in the same hurried way.

"During the delicate operation, the surgeon inadvertently severed the main artery; gangrene set in and the leg is now dead—that's why it's covered with ice. The gangrene is traveling fast. If it continues to spread at this rate without intervention, your father will die. As of this minute, he has probably about one hour, or two at best, to live—unless the leg is amputated within that time."

This was too much for me to digest in so little time. Needless to say, the unexpected devastating news shocked me to a point of stupor. But, as in the past during difficult times, the "gentle voice" in my head made its presence known again: "Take a deep breath, Luba! You need to be strong for your father's sake, and for your mother, too. Be grateful that even under these trying circumstances, you're not alone. You have Sister ——- to guide you every step of the way. Look upon her as your Guardian Angel here on earth—God's Messenger of Mercy to help you get through this. Now, stand up straight, and listen carefully to the one standing next to you." Of course, it was Sister ——- who continued giving me the instructions in her effort to help save my father's life.

"Call the surgeon who operated on your father—here is his number—as soon as I am finished talking to you! Tell him to get to the hospital with a specialist, immediately, and amputate your father's leg!" this precious human being, God's messenger, ordered, and went on. "Stress to him you know what led to this tragedy. Also tell him you and your mother will take legal action (I wasn't even aware such things as "legal action" were possible) if no attempt is made to save your father's life. Under no circumstances reveal the source of your information. Seek me out if things are not going according to plan. Don't waste time on self-pity—hurry!" she blurted, and disappeared before I could even say "thank you." I did exactly as I was instructed.

The doctor was in his office when I called—I spoke to him directly. He agreed to come to the hospital with a specialist, without delay. Meanwhile, he called ahead to a blood bank and requested 0 negative blood, which my father would need during and after his life-saving surgery. I was instructed by the surgeon to pick up and deliver the blood to the hospital via a taxi, immediately. I, of course, did. Within an hour or two my father's leg was amputated, unfortunately very high on the thigh, leaving no stump what so ever. Following the amputation, he remained on the critical list for weeks on end, in and out of the coma; his temperature spiraling as high as 106 degrees F.

After two to three months in the hospital in and out of consciousness, many more operations to stop the ongoing infections, hemorrhage from the base of the hip where the leg was amputated and many touch and go moments, he was finally discharged from the hospital. A kindly, strapping young neighbor carried him up to our third-floor apartment.

172

Looking back, I remember many sleepless nights in the hospital by my father's bedside while he was fighting for his life, keeping vigil over him and reflecting on his never-to-be-forgotten motto: "Save for the rainy day because sooner or later it will come." Without any insurance to fall back on, this was truly a "rainy day," and a continuation of it that went on and on for the remainder of my father's life.

In reality, in addition to the professional nursing staff, my mother and I were constantly at my father's side during his long hospitalization, tending to his every need, embracing him with unconditional love and urging him to fight to live because we loved him and needed him.

Now, this hard-working, talented person—my father—was an invalid. A broken man, whose dreams and ambitions were mercilessly cut short, and whose working days were over at age fifty-two, when he was at the peak of his career. To help with the mounting bills, my mother went to work. She cleaned offices at a local bank. I subsidized her meager income with half of my salary. I also took over the household responsibilities my father was no longer able to handle. Life seemed so unfair, so unpredictable. I remembered the time—regretfully—when I resented my parents for spending too much time with each other and neglecting me. Now I was crying for them, because their quality time together after they were reunited was so short. Only a few seasons of blooming petunias.

Once at home, no longer plagued by periods of unconsciousness and with idle time on his hands, the reality of exactly what had happened to him in the hospital hit my father hard! The realization of his profound disability plunged him into a deep depression, panic, and self-pity, causing confusion and disorder for all of us—at times beyond what my mother and I were able to handle. Two of many similar incidents are related below:

In a desperate need of pain medication one night, my father braved a walk, using his newly acquired crutches for the first time, in search of a pain pill. When he couldn't find it, he decided to walk to where my mother and I were sleeping peacefully—a rare blessing for us at the time—to ask for it. Still unsteady on his crutches, he slipped and fell. Fearing the worse on the way down, he screamed at the top of his lungs for help. My mother jumped to her feet and ran in his direction. She found him flat on the wooden floor, his crutches pointing in different directions, moaning. I too jumped to my feet but didn't get very far. I passed out cold from the shock before I reached what must have been one pathetic-looking scene—my frightened-half-to-death mother running from one outstretched body to another, not knowing the condition of either. Fortunately, this episode had a happy ending. Besides a few bruises and black-and-blue spots more on my father's body than on mine—we were both fine, thanks to my courageous mother.

On another occasion, I invited a few friends from the church choir—of which I was a member at the time and remain a devoted Church member to-date (Eastern Orthodox Church)—for light refreshments and fellowship following the usual Friday-evening rehearsal. My parents were aware I had company coming. My father was especially happy that I was finally resuming my own life again, and even helped with the preparations for this special occasion, my mother told me afterwards. That evening, while I was entertaining my friends from the church choir, my father—out of the blue—went ballistic, according to my mom:

"Luba, please don't have anyone to the house again. Not as long as your father's condition remains unchanged," my mother pleaded before she explained herself.

"While you were entertaining your guests in the kitchen and were having fun, I had your father pinned down on the bed and held him down with all my might the entire time because he wanted to chase everybody out with his crutches," my mom revealed, her eyes swollen from crying and her hands shaking. I too had a news flash for her:

"My evening was far from pleasant," I confessed to my mother. "I heard some kind of struggling coming from my father's room, so I knew something unpleasant was going on, but was afraid to find out while my friends were having fun. In reality, I was glad they were kind of loud, because their laughter drowned out the noises in the background," I told my mother. Oh, but how grateful I was to my mom for saving me from probably the most hideous embarrassment of my life, especially since one fellow in the group happened to be someone

I desperately wanted to impress. It was at that moment I decided, and promised my mother, I would do everything in my power to find help for my father. I owed as much to him and to us as a family.

Miraculously, I didn't have to search far to find the help my father needed. A lady who sang with me in the church choir heard of my grim situation at home from other choir members, and graciously offered her assistance. Betty was quite a bit older than I, so there was no particular friendship between us. I didn't even know she was a nurse with expertise in the field of physical rehabilitation, and a heart as big as what this specialized area was destined to become in years to come. On her own, with our approval, Betty made all the arrangements to have my father admitted to a special facility for physical and mental rehabilitation. Seeing other severely handicapped people overcoming their disabilities through hard work and positive thinking was the incentive my father needed to set goals for himself, too. In time, he let go of the "poor me! I have to accept my lot in life" attitude and replaced it with one of possibility and hope. This new way of thinking helped him to see the light—brighter with each passing day—at the end of the dark tunnel. Eventually, he was fitted for a prosthesis and was taught how to walk again.

To free my father from being a prisoner in our third-floor apartment, we were forced to move again, this time to a home of our own. My father needed a ground-floor apartment because he could no longer navigate steps. A suitable place in the same neighborhood was put up for sale. It had a candy store on the ground floor facing the street, and two large rooms in the back of the candy store facing a garden—an answer to our prayers. My parents bought the four-story brownstone building with my father's "rainy day" savings over the years and a small compensation he received from the doctor who inadvertently caused his disability.

My father's case was settled out of court. And there would have been no compensation of any kind had not my father's attorney, who worked on his disability insurance, convinced him that he had a legitimate case according to the hospital records which he was allowed to examine.

In those days, people did not sue their doctors for malpractice or any other damages—such rare cases were kept under cover by both parties, doctors and patients. I relate this true story at this time to show how far we've come in the realm of medical justice for better and for worse since the fifties. One can only imagine how differently my father's case would have been handled today. Having said that, I wish to be put on record that I mean no disrespect towards the dedicated medical profession of today (and back then, too), when I write about my father's unfortunate case of long ago. Personally, I thank God for the wonderful dedicated doctors in my life (and in other people's lives also) who have kept me in good health all these years and hopefully will for many more. Thank you Dr. C. Wagner and all your professional associates.

In our new home, we settled into the two-room apartment facing the garden—our pride and joy and a place for me to plant my own petunia garden from which to draw inspiration and strength, like in the past. My parents operated the penny-business candy store facing the street. My mother quit her job as a cleaning lady in the bank so she'd be able to help my father in the store; they also hired a sweet young girl from the neighborhood to help them out for a few hours after school. We rented the other three apartments for extra income and kept two small bedrooms and a sizable living room above the store for our use; one room became my bedroom.

On weekends, as well as after work and evening classes on weekdays, I pitched in to give my parents a break from the tedious work of serving the public from six in the morning until ten at night, seven days a week—selling newspapers, ice cream, soda, cigarettes (smoking was fashionable then), and penny candies. I also kept their business books in order.

The "eleventh-hour" (last minute) consensus to amputate my father's leg extended his life by twenty-five years. He died at age seventy-seven. Sadly, the gift of additional years came with a hefty price not only for him, but for our whole family. Who could ever forget his constant pain and his more than fifteen operations over the years—some in the hospital, others in the doctor's office—all due to frequent infections, boils, and ongoing (at times severe) bleeding caused by constant rubbing of the rough leather basket attached to his heavy wooden prosthesis and then to his waist by special belt-contraptions, in order for him to walk again with the aid of a cane. When he removed his prosthesis (another complicated process), he used crutches. Unfortunately the technology of today in such and similar cases was not there back then.

In retrospect, my father's life as well as our family's would have been a whole lot easier had the leg been amputated just above the knee when the irreversible mistake happened in the operating room. It is my belief that, the surgeon's greatest liability occurred when he overlooked the option to amputate while the upper part of my father's leg was still free of gangrene. Even doctors can make mistakes because they are human like the rest of us.

In spite of the tragedy that befell our family, we did not stray from each other during this long period of "rainy days." In fact, the "rainy days" brought us even closer together, because we needed each other more than ever before. And we remained forever grateful for the precious additional years we had with my father—in spite of everything that went wrong!

Chapter 22

The Journey Driven by My Soul's Calling

To have kept on empowering all the "ifs" and "might have beens" following my father's medical mishap could only have led to further depletion of our waning physical and emotional resilience due to purposeless resentments. How blessed we were, especially my disabled father, to have realized this fact in time, before the overwhelming challenges destroyed his will to live and further complicated our lives along with his. How fortunate we were that, together, we faced and accepted what we couldn't change, opened up and reached out to outside help; that we didn't close our eyes to the universal truth—-where there is life there is hope! And with hope, possibilities beyond what our eyes can see.

In helping my parents in their hour of need, I learned a valuable and timely lesson also, which unfortunately evaded my mother and father during their years together, then apart, and finally together again. It was heartbreaking to listen to them lament about the missed opportunities for enjoying their short-lived sunny days together more fully than they had, because every spare penny had to be put away for that "rainy day" always lurking from the nearest hiding place. I would not let my life be dominated by the fear of the "rainy days" and let the precious moments pass me by like they did my parents, I vowed!

My work, evening classes at Seton Hall University where I studied English Lit and business, as well as assisting my parents in the "Mom and Pop" candy store on weekends, kept me very busy. But besides the daily tasks—some mundane, some enjoyable—there was always something exciting to look forward to, and I relished those special moments: buying a new dress for a Saturday-night dance; a Saturday-night date with someone I had met at a dance the week before; planning vacations to exotic places with friends from work and church; corresponding with John who was in the army, stationed in Korea. I looked forward to John's letters with immense pleasure and always answered them promptly, on the pretense that I simply wanted to do my part in support of a lonely soldier—and a good friend—far away from home. And when my friends alluded there was more between John and me than mere friendship, I would always deny it. Time proved me wrong! My friends told the truth when they said they saw stars in my eyes every time I spoke of my "good friend" John. Life was good again, and I savored that period of my youth, even though several broken hearts managed to sneak into those otherwise happy years. By the same token, I too broke a few unsuspecting hearts—probably just as many as I experienced. But, like F. E. Smedley wrote in 1850—"All's fair in love and war," no matter how painful.

I loved the trip to Puerto Rico with girlfriends from work, and the never-to-be-forgotten trip to the west coast, enjoying the spectacular views of California's golden hills and the world-renowned Golden Gate Bridge from the trolley-car window; the rejuvenating vacation I spent in the beautiful resort called Vacation Valley in the Pocono Mountains in Pennsylvania, with a girlfriend from church. All this was well and good. But I never returned to the place I wanted to visit most—my beloved Carpathian Mountains where I was born and raised.

Like the silvery salmon swimming hundreds of miles in pursuit of their place of birth before they die, I needed to go back to the place of my birth, too—not to die, but to live life more fully in my beloved adopted country of America. I needed to see for myself what had happened to everything we left behind when we were forced out—our home, our beautiful meadows and forest—which I thought as a child was the beginning and the end of the whole world.

At the age of twenty-four (1957), I was financially and emotionally ready to take the solo journey to the place of my birth. My brother Michael, now married with a family of his own, still lived in the western part of Poland, in the same house we settled in after the forced deportation from our ancestral home in the Carpathian Mountains in 1947. Brother John, meanwhile, was already in America by then, living and working in Cleveland, Ohio.

John arrived shortly after our father's unsuccessful surgery and lived at home only for a brief time. He accepted a managerial position in a "Lemko Club" in Cleveland, Ohio, where he could make use of his fluency in several Slavic languages, mainly Lemko-Rusyn, Ukrainian and Polish, since he spoke no English. It was sad to see him go so soon after finally joining us in America, but to keep him back would have been selfish. In his early thirties, he needed a place of his own as well as a job with a future, and the one in Cleveland seemed to offer both.

When John left for Cleveland, we comforted ourselves with the thought that there were no oceans separating us and we could always visit back and forth and keep in touch via the telephone, which we did. My mother and I took several thirteen-hour bus trips to visit John in Cleveland, but my father visited him only once. Traveling long distances, even by plane—which he did, dragging his heavy prosthesis, was very difficult for him; also the bond between father and son was not what each expected and hoped for—probably due to many years of separation. Nonetheless, John spent every vacation and every major holiday with us. He would come home loaded with special gifts for everyone, especially at Christmastime. Blessed by good business sense, he took advantage of his God-given talent, combined it with hard work, and achieved the American dream. He eventually returned to his home base in Jersey City where the rest of our family had settled; he remained single. One of the happiest moments of his life was when he received his American Citizenship. I know; I was there and saw for myself the joy in his eyes when this precious document was handed to him, and afterwards when, as a family, we celebrated this special occasion to honor John on becoming an American citizen.

As if in a dream, I found myself crossing the continent again. This time—eight years later—I was flying in the opposite direction, to visit the land of my humble beginnings. Influenced by the American way of life and education, I felt like an American and, I believe, I looked like one, too. Dressed in trendy fashion and fluent

180

in the English language, I felt confident on the inside as well as on the outside—with only a trace of accent, which made me stand out then and still does today. Yet, on some level, I was then and still am today that young peasant girl whose roots remained buried deep in the soil of the Carpathian Mountains. The expression "You can take the boy (in this case a girl) out of the country, but you can't take the country out of the boy (a girl)," still defines who I am today.

My first stop on the way to my "Lemkovyna" was to visit my brother Michael and his family—my sister-in-law, a young nephew and three little nieces. My new sister-in-law happened to be our former neighbor in the Carpathian Mountains and the sister of my brother Michael's best friend, Wasyl, who vanished in the Second World War, so I recognized her immediately. But my nephew and nieces—the blessed additions to our family—I met for the first time. I could hardly believe my eyes: These four precious little ones belonged to our family. To me they represented a gift that could surpass no other. Oh, how I wished my parents—their grandparents—could have been there to share this joy with me! My wish was not in vain! Several years later, it became a reality for all of us.

My brother Michael did not recognize me, perhaps because my visit was kept a secret from him and his family. When I reached his village—my former home in exile—via a train I boarded near the Warsaw airport, I introduced myself to the station attendant and pleasantly discovered he was a friend of my brother's. The attendant suggested that we play a little trick on Michael—a harmless joke in the name of friendship. He sent a messenger for Michael on the pretense there was a special delivery for him from America requiring immediate pickup. Michael hurried to the station. Meanwhile the attendant had another suggestion to further confuse my unsuspecting brother. "Hide here and when I give you the signal walk past Michael and we'll watch for his reaction." I did as instructed, trusting in the attendant's better judgment. When I passed by Michael, he glanced at me and rubbed his eyes as if suddenly he was seeing things he shouldn't be seeing. Twice more I strutted passed my brother, who now appeared confused to the core, still rubbing his eyes. That's when I decided the station attendant had had enough fun at my brother's expense. And he, too, must have felt some compassion for Michael. Carrying my two suitcases and grinning from ear to ear, he stopped at my brother's side at the same moment that I did—happy tears smudging my carefully applied makeup. The lightbulb in my brother's head finally went on! Oh, how I wish there had been such a thing as a present-day video camera, so our one-of-a-kind reunion, could have been taped and saved. Sadly, except for my memories of that extraordinary moment—and hopefully Michael's during his lifetime (he died at age fifty-five)—our special reunion is lost to posterity, along with priceless others.

"You looked so familiar, but who you were I didn't know. You grew up so beautifully!" Michael later acknowledged.

I was glad for the foresight to pack lots of chocolate bars, packages of flavored gum, dolls, and several toy trucks for the little ones. After all, I was the rich auntie from America—the land of plenty! And they were right about the "land of plenty," but very wrong about the "rich auntie" part. Nonetheless, I was looked upon as an honored guest not only by my family but everyone in the immediate vicinity— one worthy of respect—as I soon found out. To my surprise, I was asked to be the Maid of Honor at a wedding of a former girlfriend's sister I barely remembered.

With only two weeks of vacation time from work, giving up three days for the elaborate wedding of an acquaintance troubled me, but not to the point of refusal. The wedding was exceptional, the kind we middle-class folks in America would never attempt to duplicate, for obvious reasons. It began on a Sunday morning with a processional from the bride's parents' home to church—accompanied by a band headed by my brother Michael (an accordionist with his own band)— where the bride met her soon to be husband. The bride dressed in the traditional white wedding gown with the long veil trailing behind her, and the wedding party, including the groom, wore their Sunday attire, enhanced by a bunch of flowers tied with long ribbons pinned to the groom's and groomsmen's lapels, and to the bridesmaid's dresses.

Back from church to the bride's parents' house, the reception began. And it lasted one-and-a-half days before moving on to the groom's parents' house for another day-and-a-half to continue the celebration in the same fashion. There was nonstop music, dancing, and singing in all the rooms of the house, devoid of larger pieces of furniture. Delicious homemade foods were being served on and off throughout the day and night, prepared by the—specially hired for the occasion—ladies. The first night, after midnight, I saw a few people leaving for home, probably to get some much needed sleep and then come back to continue celebrating. I decided to do the same and quietly slipped away from the table—via the space under the table—and out the door, since I knew making my exit obvious was not an option, as my brother and sister-in-law had warned.

No sooner did I get home—a few houses down the road from the wedding reception—and made myself comfortable in the featherbed, than as if in a dream the entire bridal party, including the bride and groom, appeared before me. I was bodily removed from bed and carried back to the wedding reception in my pajamas—my dress, shoes, and undergarments being carried by one of the bridesmaids, who helped me quickly get dressed again and escorted me back to the bridal table. The next time I slept again was when my brother Michael needed to catch some sleep, and this time I slept fully dressed. I was glad when this unforgettable wedding finally ended at the groom's parents' home—three days later—and I could get a few hours of uninterrupted sleep, as well as spend some quality time with my newly discovered family before I began the long journey to my "Lemkovyna," thankfully accompanied by my brother Michael and young nephew Roman, old enough to tolerate the rigorous journey to our ancestral village of Liszczyny in the Carpathian Mountains.

The sleepless night in a rickety train was the beginning of the grueling physical and emotional journey back home. It was noontime on a hot July day when we reached the remote area where once our village had brimmed with life and was now desolate. I was grateful I had my brother and his son with me. Without them, I probably would never have found my way through the overgrown, rugged mountain terrain to the village.

In my time, there were well-defined paths leading to the village from various mountain ranges, forested areas and meadows. And I knew them well—once upon a time. These paths were clearly marked by the constant trudging of humans and domestic animals, and were now obliterated by time and the absence of both. It was over those mountains I so often ran to get our mail from the village of Losie, where the post office was. And I was never afraid, even when the way home was lit by the moon and the stars only.

On one such occasion, I mailed a letter to my father and there happened to be a letter from him, too. The envelope seemed kind of thick, so my curiosity got the best of me. I shouldn't have opened it, but I did. It was my birthday and although we didn't celebrate birthdays as such at the time, I thought how nice it would be if there was something in that thick envelope for me too, and not just a letter of many pages for my mother. And there was, much to my surprise and joy. In addition to a lengthy letter, there was a postcard with my name on it, enhanced by a lovely drawing of a bouquet of roses on one side. Attached to the back of it was a gold cross on a gold chain, honoring my May birthday.

I tore the cross off of the postcard, clasped it around my neck and ran home as fast as my legs could carry me, to show off my unexpected treasure to everyone I knew. To this day, I still remember that joyful moment and myself as a young peasant girl who was convinced she was the luckiest thirteen-year-old in the whole world. No other girl I knew could claim she had a father in a faraway land called America, who loved her just because he was her Daddy, in spite of the fact that in her mind he was more an image than a real person. That cross has been my constant companion ever since. Without it I feel incomplete.

From the top of the mountain we saw what we were about to find in the village—half-standing houses and overgrown lots where others once stood. Overwhelmed by what we saw from afar, we trudged on with hearts as heavy as heaps of rocks. Soon we were in our once-lively village—now devoid of people. Tearfully, we continued on through the overgrown, barely visible country road, which once served as the main thoroughfare to and from our village, until we reached the approximate place where once stood our ancestral home, enhanced by two stately oak trees. When I realized I was standing on that very spot, I reached for my brother's hand. Together, we bowed our heads in sad remembrance and reverence to the sacred ground which had supported the humble log home where countless members of our family were born, lived out their lives, and died. A heap of rocks collected by my father over the years, which were to serve as a foundation for a new and larger home for our family, to be built on another lot of our land, remained intact. It was the only thing that I recognized. Even the dainty forget-me-not blue flowers were still growing at the base of the never-to-be-used-as-intended, pile of rocks. As a child I had picked those delicate blue beauties and made tiny bouquets out of them to decorate the Holy Icons in our home, in front of which we said our prayers every morning and evening.

Overwhelmed by the ghostly feeling permeating throughout the village, but still linked in my mind to the lives of the people who once lived there, we trudged on. We reached our final destination at the cement monument in the shape of a cross with our family name engraved at its base. I remembered decorating the Cross with wild-flowers every spring, summer and fall, and I wanted to do the same on the occasion of my return, this time with a bunch of forget-me-nots I picked at the base of the moss-covered hill of rocks near our—now gone—homestead. I was about to uproot a few clusters of wild grass to make room for the flowers when Michael grabbed my hand and pulled me away from the Cross. Wrapped around the base of the Cross were two huge snakes sunning themselves, and I hadn't seen them. Were they poisonous? We had no way of knowing, but a snake is still a snake and not to be trusted or fooled around with. In my case especially, since I was deathly afraid of snakes ever since my one and only encounter with a snake, referred to in Chapter 14 of this book.

We had plans to walk on the land as well as in the forest to visit the nooks and crannies of our childhood and expose my nephew to a brief family history related to the areas we covered, but changed our minds. We realized our land was no longer ours. It now belonged to nature and its wild creatures. The land which sustained us for generations had returned to the wilderness our predecessors found when they settled in the Carpathian Mountains many centuries ago.

Exhausted, hungry and overcome by the chaos we found, we stopped at the home of dear cousins (Irena and Staszek)—one of the two families fortunate not to have been thrown out of their homes, probably due to intermarriage. We were welcomed with open arms and invited to spend the night with them before moving on. Their exceptional hospitality took the edge off of our physical and emotional upheavals and refueled our bodies for the equally grueling return journeys—my brother and nephew to their home in the western part of Poland and me to mine in America.

Before we left the village early the next morning, we stopped at the cemetery to pay respect to our departed loved ones. We especially wanted to place flowers at the resting place of our baby sister, but the tall wild grasses and the desecration of the graves in that area prevented us from finding it. We did, however, find the graves of our grandparents on both sides, said our prayers there and placed flowers on each of their gravestones.

We moved on to the grossly neglected and forgotten old wooden church on the hill, near the village cemetery we had just visited. We stood for a moment in front of the locked door, being careful, as at the cemetery, not to inadvertently step on a curled up snake or a bunch of them, prevalent throughout the village. We said a silent prayer and reflected briefly on the times we both remembered well, when we sang praises to God in that once well-taken-care-of edifice, every Sunday morning and on Holy Days. Now the only voices still heard were those of the birds nesting in the missing shingles. From there, hand in hand, we left the village. I whispered good-bye as I glanced back at the remains of our village from the top of the mountain—for the last and final time. I was sure!

"How sad one cannot go home again," I heard my brother say under his breath.

"Home is where your heart is, Michael," I replied, hoping in some way to comfort my brother as well as myself. "And your heart is where your loved ones are. Once upon a time our loved ones were here and so were our hearts; now that time is gone. But we will always have our memories of that time, and that's what we must treasure and never forget," I recited in monotone, causing another flood of tears—not only for me and my brother, but also his young son, my nephew—even though he probably didn't understand the reason for so much sadness.

Back in the city of Gorlice, to catch trains to different destinations—Michael and young Roman to their home in exile, and I to the plane that would carry me back to mine—over the ocean where my parents, friends, and a job were waiting for me, we said our farewells but not good-bye. "Until we meet in America," we whispered to each other.

In America, where my life was waiting for me with my soul mate, John! Where God intended us to spend a lifetime together and bless us with two beautiful, most loving daughters, Kyra Ann and Laura Jean. Where our—superb in every way in our eyes—four grandchildren, would be born: Kyra's and Christopher's two handsome sons, Adam John and Christopher Michael. Laura's and Jonathan's two beautiful daughters, Kara Frances and Faith Anastasia. Where my brother Michael and his family would eventually come and complete our family circle.

Today I wonder: would any of these extraordinary blessings be possible, had there not been Blossoms on a Rooftop in my life?

May there always be a window overlooking your own garden of blossoms of inspiration as you journey on…through life!